Social Work and Spirituality

Social Work and Spirituality

IAN MATHEWS

Series Editors: Jonathan Parker and Greta Bradley

First published in 2009 by Learning Matters Ltd

British Library Cataloguing in Publication Data

A CIP record for this book is available from the British Library

ISBN 978 1 84445 194 4

Cover design by Topics – The Creative Partnership
Project management by Deer Park Productions, Tavistock
Typeset by PDQ Typesetting Ltd
Printed and bound in Great Britain by Bell & Bain Ltd, Glasgow

Learning Matters Ltd
33 Southernhay East
Exeter EX1 1NX
Tel: 01392 215560
info@learningmatters.co.uk
www.learningmatters.co.uk

Contents

Acknowledgements

I owe a debt of thanks to many people for their assistance in the production of this book. Firstly I need to thank the series editor, Jonathan Parker, and Kate Lodge and Luke Block at Learning Matters, for their patient support over the many months that this book has taken to appear. I am sure that you must, on more than one occasion, have given up hope of seeing anything, so thank you for not saying so!

Secondly, as I look out of my office window across the dappling waters of the Brayford Pool, up to the spire of Lincoln Cathedral glinting in the sunshine, I am reminded that I need to thank my colleagues in the social work team at the University of Lincoln for their support and encouragement. I also know that my life would be in mortal danger if I did not mention my fantastic students on the University of Lincoln's social work degree programme. Individually and collectively they have endeavoured to drive me round the bend, but that is to be accepted as an occupational hazard. I love you all and life would not be the same without you.

Finally to Moyra, Timothy and Helena who now have the additional burden of living with a published author. Thank you for being so special to me.

Introduction

Over the last few months as I have been writing this book, religion and spirituality have rarely been out of the news. We have, for example, seen employers attempt to sack or discipline staff for displaying religious symbols. The security services, both in Britain and overseas, continue to monitor religious extremists who seek to promote or engage in acts of terrorism. And the NHS has recently generated lively debate in the media following a decision to suspend a nurse who offered to pray with a patient.

We also live in a rapidly changing pluralistic society where some of the major religious faiths seem to becoming increasingly entrenched and hostile towards one another. Christianity appears to be a declining force in society whilst other faiths seem to be growing in influence and voice. Coupled with these changes, there has been a significant increase in the number of people who are happy to identify themselves as being of no religion. Although we may note in passing, that this does not necessarily imply that they are without faith or lack spirituality.

Social work, on the other hand often seems to be oblivious to the debate which rages around it. A discussion of the role of religion or spirituality rarely features within the profession and it could be argued that there is ambivalence, even hostility, towards such an engagement. I appreciate that this is a strong statement and would want to acknowledge the contribution of pioneers such as Bernard Moss and Peter Gilbert who have consistently argued for the inclusion of spirituality in social work. Nonetheless, there is an element of truth that other professions, such as nursing and psychology, have considered the implications of spirituality in a far more explicit and consistent way. Despite its' claim to be a pioneer of holistic approaches social work has often failed to engage with those core beliefs that shape who we are as people, which we choose to define in a shorthand way as religion and spirituality.

To a large extent, that is why I have chosen to write this book. I would argue that social work is impoverished because of its lack of engagement with spirituality and that social workers need to have an awareness of both their own spirituality and the spirituality of those whom they work with. My intention is to stimulate debate through the provision of an introductory text which will hopefully encourage you to explore further; a feature of this book is that I make a number of suggestions at the end of each chapter as to where you might go next to increase your knowledge.

You may find that the journey is a challenge and that there are elements of the book that you understand easily and others that you find a struggle. Perhaps that is true of all books which seek to explore ideas which are not easy to grasp. Either way, I trust that you enjoy the challenge and that you feel that the journey is worthwhile and one of discovery.

Chapter synopsis

In Chapter 1 you will begin the journey by exploring a diverse range of definitions of spirituality. In particular, you will consider the differences and similarities between religion and spirituality. As you will discover, they are not the same. I introduce you to the idea of the human spirit and how this informs the various definitions and nuances of spirituality. The second part of the chapter begins to grapple with the question why is spirituality of importance to contemporary social work. After all, don't we live in an increasingly secular society where professional social work is seen as being a rational, evidence-based activity? Possibly we do. But at the core of social work is a working relationship between two people which has a number of spiritual overtones. Finally, you examine the historical and contemporary role of religion in social care provision and discuss the ambivalence of social work towards belief.

Chapter 2 builds on the introductory themes of the first chapter. In particular, you begin to tease out the significance of culture and the way it provides a framework for both social work and spirituality. You then progress to consider the differing roles and experiences of men and women and their understanding of spirituality. In some ways, these early chapters set the scene for the more focused discussion which subsequently follows. As always it is important to understand the context in which social work operates.

Chapter 3 introduces you to the important subject of community and spirituality. Often we view social work as being an activity which takes place with individual service users and their immediate family. We forget that individuals live in communities which exert a significant influence, for good or bad, on the person. In recent years there has been a renewed interest in the significance of community and I encourage you to explore the idea that communities can be 'spiritually bankrupt' or 'spiritually healthy'. This is by no means a linear, clear cut distinction and, as always, I would ask you to take a critical approach to your reading. You then consider the communal expression of spirituality. Again, we often think of spiritual expression or religious observance as being a private individual activity. As you will see, this is a simplistic understanding of spiritual expression as whole communities can have spirituality. Finally, you begin to make a connection between spirituality and social change. In particular, the innovative use of the arts in promoting change and transformation.

In Chapter 4 the pattern of the book changes as we begin to consider discrete areas of social work. I choose to start by looking at older people and spirituality as it allows us to consider several aspects of spirituality which are of importance to all service user groups. For example, the importance of relationships, the use of good communication skills, the experience of change and loss, and the increasing use of holistic assessment.

Chapter 5 looks at disability and spirituality. I argue that people with disabilities have been ignored or viewed in stereotypical ways throughout history and that their spiritual needs have often been neglected. Using this argument as a stimulus I then make some observations about individual and organisational practice which are designed to assist an evaluation of your own practice.

In Chapter 6 you are asked to focus on mental distress and spirituality. Spirituality has become a significant driver in mental health services over recent years and some service users find it meaningful to define their experiences in spiritual terms. There have been many connections between mental illness and spirituality; sometimes these connections have been healthy and on other occasions they have been unhelpful and oppressive. You explore these nuances as well as considering an alternative model of explanation for mental ill health–spiritual dislocation. You then spend some time thinking about spiritual assessment. Increasingly, the assessment of spirituality is a feature of holistic work where the individual needs and perspectives of the service user are recorded and considered. As throughout the book, I encourage you to think about practice issues. How can these issues be incorporated into practice and how can social workers respond to expressed spiritual need.

In Chapter 7, attention focuses on children and spirituality. In recent years, there has been an increased interest in the spiritual lives of children. Regrettably, one reason for this has been a recognition that many children live impoverished lives in Britain despite, or perhaps because of, increasing affluence and prosperity. In this chapter you start by thinking about the spiritual world of the child and how this might be expressed. You then explore what factors might adversely affect childhood spirituality and note the corrosive effect of abuse and neglect on children. You then use *Every Child Matters* to focus your thoughts on ways in which children may be helped to express their spirituality. I suggest some tools which you may consider using and we conclude by considering children within the public care system.

In some ways I am unhappy with the compartmentalisation of the book as it implies that there are more differences than commonalities when we consider spirituality. To a degree there are, but you will find that you return to the same themes and issues time and again. That is because all people, regardless of age, race, ethnicity, gender or ability have spiritual needs which social workers need to recognise and understand.

Learning features

This book is interactive and you have a responsibility to engage as an active participant in your own learning. I have included a range of case studies, vignettes and exercises which I hope you will find interesting and informative. These exercises are intended to illustrate and exemplify key points, reinforce learning and provoke debate. You will also be provided with summaries of key research and theoretical ideas, as well as suggestions for further study.

You will be expected to reflect creatively on your own learning needs and to consider how your practice can be improved as a result of your reflection. For reflection which does not produce tangible change is of no use to you or to service users.

You will note that each chapter is prefaced by reference to the National Occupational Standards and the social work subject benchmark statements which will be considered within that chapter. Some of you will be students studying for your social work degree and will anxiously have an eye on the various standards as you progress with your studies and placements. Qualified practitioners may be more relaxed about the key roles but nonetheless recognise that they serve to remind us that social work is a structured, thoughtful activity.

Chapter 1
What is spirituality?

Introduction

I wonder if you have ever grappled with a word or an idea which is commonly used and widely understood, but is difficult to pin down and define. Words like 'community' or 'care' might fall into this category as we all know what they mean but when we begin to explore them they become more elusive.

Spirituality could be considered such a word and it will require some clear thinking and hard work over the next few chapters if we are to gain a fuller understanding of its many meanings and nuances.

I think that the best place to start is with your own experience.

ACTIVITY 1.1

I want you to spend a few moments thinking about yourself and your life. Make a list of those experiences, beliefs and places which you think may have a spiritual element or relate to spirituality. You might find it helpful to write down your ideas on a piece of paper under the three headings I have suggested. Think broadly about your life and don't be afraid to write about things which may seem offbeat or not strictly relevant.

Comment

How did you get on? I did not find this exercise easy and I imagine that some of you found it difficult as well.

Here is my list:

Experiences

- Receiving help and support from both friends and strangers at difficult times in my life.

- Seeing my children born and being made aware of the beauty and fragility of life.

- Experiencing the power of nature in storm, wind and rain.

- Experiencing dreams and visions.

Beliefs

- I believe in God.

- I believe in the search for economic and social justice, especially through fair trade.

- I believe that all people are equal.

- I believe that all people have a spirituality and have a right to express it in different ways and in freedom.

Places

- My local place of worship is important to me as a source of friendship and learning.

- The hills and mountains remind me of the beauty of creation and provide me with stillness and quiet.

- I find Stonehenge inspiring and mysterious.

- Being on a boat surrounded by the sea reminds me of my small place in the universe.

Did your list look very different to mine? You might have been surprised to see some of the things I have mentioned and wondered why I included mountains, night-time dreams and those values that shape who we are as people. Don't worry too much if you feel a little lost at the moment – there is a long way to go on our journey and spirituality is a topic where there are many different responses, all of them equally valid.

In this chapter we are going to start and end by considering the role of religion. I want to be clear with you that this book is not about religion. It is about spirituality, and that is different to religion. Consequently, I am not intending to give you an in-depth understanding of religion, rather more a thumbnail sketch by way of introduction.

Religion and spirituality

I wonder what comes to mind when you think about the term religion? I imagine that many of you instinctively thought about the major religions of the world – Christianity, Islam and Judaism – and the influence they have on the world. Of course there are many more smaller religious groups, some of them very new, which you may also have considered. So what characterises a religion and how does it differ from spirituality?

I think that religions and religious groups share some of the following characteristics.

- All are based on a well-structured and organised set of beliefs. There is often debate about the nature of these core beliefs and they may evolve over time, but nonetheless adherence to them is required if you are to become a member. Frequently, beliefs will be based on teachings and rituals which are set down in holy books, such as the Talmud or the Koran.

- These beliefs differ between religions of course, but share a common theme – a belief that there is a spiritual realm beyond our own physical world which exercises an influence on the affairs of the world. Within this understanding there is, or are, a Divine Being or Beings who exemplify justice, power, love and truth.

- Crucially, these beliefs are shared by a number of people, sometimes millions of people across the world. This gives a strong communal element to religion and you may have experience of a faith where it is an expectation that believers will meet together to sing, pray, discuss or purely enjoy the company of like-minded people. Often these religious beliefs are of huge significance to the individual. They do not merely inform or influence a person's understanding of themselves and the world; they become the very driving force behind their existence. As such, they give purpose, meaning, satisfaction and structure to many millions of people.

Spirituality is at the heart of religion. The shared rites, traditions and rituals of religion, as well as the use of worship, song, dance and prayer all draw us out and away from ourselves and into a different spiritual realm.

But religion is separate to spirituality. It is merely one way of expressing spirituality, and it is not essential to be a member of a faith group in order to have or to express spirituality.

The human spirit

At the core of any thinking about spirituality is the word *spirit*. I am sure that you must be familiar with the word because it is used often in everyday conversation. For example, if we feel positive and happy about ourselves we say that we are 'in good spirits'. If a team is working well and in harmony we say that it 'has a good team spirit'. If we are making the best of adversity or a difficult situation 'we are keeping up our spirits'. The converse is true of course, and there are a number of more negative connotations connected to the word spirit – low in spirit, lacking in spirit and mean-spirited.

So the word 'spirit' is used in everyday language. It has also been a key concept in religious and philosophical thought for thousands of years.

RESEARCH SUMMARY

Gilbert (2006) provides a very helpful list of some of the different ways in which the word 'spirit' has been defined.

- *The Ancient Greeks used the word* pneuma *to describe air, breath and spirit. They believed that the body, mind, spirit and heart are all interdependent, a view that is becoming increasingly common in holistic ways of working and one which we will be exploring later.*
- *The Hebrew language uses the word ru'ach which means both breath and the core spirit of every person, which belongs to God and returns to Him at death.*
- *In Latin, the word* spiritus *is used. This can mean a number of things: breath, the human soul and vigour. This is where the English word spirit comes from and immediately reminds us of some of the phrases we used earlier.*

As you can see, there are a number of common themes that we can identify within these definitions. For example, all of them indicate that the spirit is integral to the well-being of the person, much like breath or oxygen. It is so intrinsic to our well-being that we could not live or thrive without it.

Different definitions of spirituality

While religious and philosophical ideas from past times are helpful in developing our understanding, we need to consider some more contemporary definitions which will help us in our quest.

The first definition of spirituality (the human spirit) I want you to consider comes from the National Institute for Mental Health in England (NIMHE), an organisation that facilitates change in mental health services.

It can refer to the essence of human beings as unique individuals, what makes me, me & you, you.

So it is the power, energy & hopefulness in a person.

It is what is deepest in us – what gives us direction, motivation. It is what enables a person to survive bad times, to overcome difficulties, to be themselves.

(NIMHE, 2003)

A similar definition is provided by Slay (2007) who suggests that:

[S]pirituality [is] the expression of a person's humanity, whatever it is that helps to shape that person, & the well of inner strength from which that person draws support at time of crisis.

I am sure that you will have noted the connections between these definitions and some of the older ideas we previously considered. There is an emphasis on the spirit as being what defines who we are as people, what makes us unique as people. It is also a source of power, inspiration and drive – what moves us forward in life and what enables us to overcome difficulty.

I don't want to overly burden you with different definitions as this may only confuse you. What I would like you to do is to try and work out a definition of spirituality for yourself. In order to help you to do this, I want to look now at some of the many characteristics of spirituality, using the definitions we have considered as a starting point.

Meaning and purpose

So what is spirituality? Firstly I want to suggest that spirituality is what gives meaning and purpose to our lives. The gift of purpose and meaning is very precious and some-times in social work you will come across people who lead lives that seem devoid of both. How people achieve a sense of purpose and meaning is highly individualistic. Some will see themselves as having a major goal in life which they are working towards. Others will have a gift, maybe music, art, language, writing, acting or sport-ing ability, which is extremely important to them and defines who they are as people. Some may find meaning in having a specific role or relationship – parent, friend, social worker, doctor or nurse for example. Still more will achieve meaning through personal faith or adherence to a particular political or philosophical position.

If you like, it is what makes us tick as people, what motivates us to carry on in life, what compels us to get out of bed every morning. This may well be a combination of things which could, and will, change over time, almost from day to day. They will be highly individualistic and will be those roles, relationships, attributes and gifts that we hold most dear and define who we are as people.

In passing, it is important to note that achieving a sense of meaning and purpose by gaining a role can be dependent on factors beyond your immediate control. For example, you may be an extremely gifted musician but if your family are too poor to purchase a musical instrument or to send you to music lessons, this may well impact on your musical development. Equally, if you are a gifted sports person but sustain a bad injury, it is possible that this will end your career. Or if you attend a poorly-performing/failing school with limited aspirations it may be difficult for you to go to university or to undertake professional training. This is an important consideration as many people in our society are unable to achieve their full potential due to social exclusion, poverty and the effects of a range of oppressions such as racism, ageism and homophobia.

How we view the world

Another important aspect of spirituality is an understanding of those core beliefs which enable us to make sense of the world and the events that shape our lives. The world is often a baffling place where things happen over which we have little or no control. Some people may believe that God is in control while others may believe in fate – what will be, will be. Yet others believe in the ability of humanity to dominate the planet while others believe that the forces of nature or 'Mother Earth' ultimately decide the affairs of men and women.

Our beliefs concerning the world and how it operates help us to find answers to those questions in life with which we all struggle: Why has this happened to me? What more could I have done? Where am I going? How can I make things better? How we make sense of the world and gain a sense of security is important to all of us who work in health and social care. For how can we support vulnerable people who are at a point of crisis in their lives if we have never struggled to find answers to uncertainty and doubt? As Lloyd (1997) points out, practitioners are often working with people whose lives are characterised by loss and distress. If we do not feel comfortable addressing the question 'Why has this happened?' we will not be able to provide a holistic, professional service when it is most needed.

Spirituality and values

Spirituality is not only about our worldview and what gets us out of bed in the morning, but also what guides our behaviour for the rest of the day. For spirituality is directly related to our value base: those beliefs, values and morals which are integral to us and from which we will not deviate. Put another way, it is our moral code or moral compass. Again, these positions may be informed by religious belief or they may be entirely secular. For example, in social work we emphasise such values as choice, empowerment, dignity, respect, anti-oppressive practice and so on. These could be seen as the spiritual basis of social work.

Spirituality and relationships

So far you may be thinking that spirituality is very much a private affair, something which is unique and personal to each individual. While this may be true, there is another dimension that we need to consider.

Moss (2005) begins to tease out this particular aspect by posing a series of questions:

> *What difference does all of this make to you and to what you do with your life? What impact does it have upon how you treat other people both individually and within communities? (p13)*

In other words, spirituality is what we use to demonstrate our worldview in action. It is shown in how we respond to others, how we develop ties and relationships, how we demonstrate a sense of responsibility to other people and communities.

Spirituality then is not just a personal matter, it has an outward-looking dimension. It would be impertinent of me to ask why you had chosen to become a social worker or care professional. But I suspect that at least some of you chose this path because it parallels your own spiritual values and beliefs. You believe in social justice, compassion, the promotion of opportunity and the protection of those who need it, and social work is an excellent way of demonstrating those beliefs in action.

Often when I am interviewing prospective students for my social work degree course, they confess that one of the main reasons they want to enter the profession is to 'help people'. While this may demonstrate a limited understanding of the complexities of the job, it is nonetheless a positive starting point and is a good example of how we seek to demonstrate spirituality in action.

RESEARCH SUMMARY

How is spirituality expressed?
You may feel that we have already answered this question by looking at the expression of values and the importance of relationships. But I want you to see that spirituality is expressed in a number of ways, many of which are quite mundane and ordinary but are of significance nonetheless.

The Mental Health Foundation (2007) provides this list of possibilities:

- *religious practices such as worship, prayer and reading religious texts;*
- *coming together as a spiritual community;*
- *living by certain values;*
- *rituals such as burning incense;*
- *wearing particular clothes or eating particular foods;*
- *cultural or creative activities such as making music or creating art;*
- *getting closer to nature;*

$\rightarrow$

RESEARCH SUMMARY *continued*

- *activities that develop self-awareness or personal control such as contemplation or yoga;*
- *physical activity;*
- *friendship or voluntary work.*

This list is by no means exhaustive and we will be looking at more ways of expressing spirituality throughout the book.

Why is spirituality important to social work?

So far we have spent time trying to tease out the different meanings and characteristics of spirituality. Before we get any further in our exploration, however, we need to consider why we are making the journey in the first place. Why is spirituality important to social work and how does it inform and influence professional practice?

ACTIVITY **1.2**

I want you to spend some time reflecting on what you have learnt so far about spirituality. Using your own words, define spirituality and make a list of reasons why you think it is of importance to social work.

I want to suggest that spirituality is important to social work for a number of reasons.

Spirituality and better health

Firstly, there is a growing body of evidence to suggest that religious belief, belonging to a place of worship and spiritual expression is good for both physical and mental health.

Social work is increasingly concerned with health promotion and social workers work closely with colleagues from health backgrounds to promote well-being in both individuals and communities. Clearly, anything that helps in this difficult task should be of interest to us and should be encouraged.

RESEARCH SUMMARY

Koenig, et al. (2001) undertook research in America which showed that commitment to the Christian faith and the regular observance of religious rites and rituals such as attendance at church led to a number of health benefits. These included:

- *an extended life expectancy;*
- *lower blood pressure;*

→

RESEARCH SUMMARY continued

- *lower rates of death from heart disease and heart attacks;*
- *an increased success in heart transplant surgery;*
- *reduced cholesterol levels;*
- *reduced levels of pain in people with cancer.*

Comment

These results have been replicated in a number of different studies and settings. For example, a recent influential report from the Mental Health Foundation claimed that:

> ...spirituality may reduce feelings of negative emotions, such as anger, fear, and revenge, reducing tension levels. This reduction may lead to a stronger immune system, lower blood pressure and reduced risk of cardiovascular disease and strokes. For example, an individual who practises yoga is likely to experience a reduction in anxiety, depression, post traumatic stress disorder, stress and other stress related medical illnesses.

(Lindridge, 2007, p15)

Other studies have also highlighted the benefits of spiritual belief and practices to recovering from bereavement (Walsh, et al., 2002; Coleman, et al., 2002), working through the gradual loss of a loved one to dementia (Pointon, 2007) and dealing with near death issues in palliative care (Langlands, et al., 2007).

RESEARCH SUMMARY

The reasons why spiritual expression might promote better health are complex and may include the following:

- *Attendance at a place of worship increases your sense of identity and a sense of belonging. It provides company, stimulation and a reason to get up in the morning.*
- *Religious rites and rituals, such as specified times of daily prayer or a religious calendar which marks the passing of the year, provide structure and meaning to your life.*
- *Places of worship and religious groups provide practical and emotional support at times of need.*
- *Spiritual expression and getting in touch with forces and powers outside of the individual enhances psychological well-being.*
- *The view of the world promoted by spirituality gives reassurance and a measure of security in an uncertain world.*

Adapted from Chatters (2000)

You may have noticed that many of these benefits are related to identity, meaning, and belonging, all of which are crucial to a sense of who we are and how we relate to the wider world.

The inadequacy of science, logic and rationalism

Another reason why social workers need to gain an understanding of spirituality is that the profession often grapples with problems and questions where logical and scientific explanations offer little help, for example:

- the breakdown of family and personal relationships;

- abusive behaviours and experiences;

- the problem of emotional pain, separation and loss;

- wider structural issues such as community breakdown, unemployment and poverty;

- issues of oppression such as racism and homophobia;

- the influence of gender, class and education.

Often science and rational thought do not provide us with either an explanation or, more importantly, a solution to these situations. Some would argue that human life is not a rational process and that science can only ever offer inadequate and unsatisfying explanations (Tacey, 2004), so we need to look elsewhere for guidance in our practice and seek alternative explanations.

Other professions, which interestingly have more of a scientific background than social work, notably nursing, have been grappling with this issue for some years. Tanyi (2002), for example, argues that science is unable to address such issues as the search for peace and meaning, which are as important as *cure* to many patients, and that spiritual care has been an essential component of nursing for generations. This is an important point. Often when we think about nursing and medicine we envisage professionals in uniforms in busy wards with machines, procedures to follow and treatments to deliver, often in order to meet targets set by the Department of Health. While we all want efficient and modern care, there is still room for what we might call a good 'bedside manner' where time is taken to listen to the concerns and worries of patients and patients can engage with carers as fellow human beings.

Gilbert (2006) takes this argument further and suggests that as contemporary societies grapple with such events as 9/11 and the terrorist bombs in London, spiritual explanations are becoming increasingly important. Simply put, I think that Gilbert is saying that in a world which seems more divided than ever, there is an increasing need for care professionals to identify and use those common elements of humanity which we all share, as a basis for their work.

It would be clearly unwise to dismiss scientific explanation or the need for logic and rational thought in social work. After all there is an increasing demand for what is termed *evidence-based practice* where social work is asked to prove that what it does is based on solid foundations and is not merely the exercise of common sense. It would be equally foolish to suggest that spiritual ways of thinking hold the answer to all of the problems that social workers have to grapple with on a daily basis. But, I would argue, there does need to be an increased awareness of spirituality and a more holistic understanding of problem-solving.

Holistic assessment

Another reason why social work needs to take spirituality seriously is the recent emphasis on holistic assessment. With its emphasis on working with the body, mind and spirit and recognising the validity of service user experience and context, holistic ways of working have become something of a 'holy grail' in social work in recent years. It can be seen as a revolt against the managerial prominence placed on outcomes, targets and processes that have increasingly defined the profession.

Again, social work is not alone in seeking to reclaim a way of working where people and their lived experience are recognised and valued for who they are rather than for what problems they bring or for which boxes they tick. Basset and Basset (2007), who write from a nursing background, reflect on the shortcomings of their profession in the National Health Service:

> *The time is certainly right for a re-birth of spirituality. We work in a system that is perfectly at ease with itself in referring to older people who have nowhere to go and remain in hospital as 'bed blockers', and a bad day at Accident and Emergency is sometimes described as 'we had a lot of rubbish to deal with today.'*

We will be spending some time later in the book looking at holistic ways of working in more depth. What I would like you to appreciate at this early stage is that any work in the caring professions which values and promotes humanity and reinforces identity and self-worth has a spiritual aspect.

CASE STUDY

Sandy, a woman of Indian descent who has a nominal Buddhist background, was admitted to hospital with a terminal illness. It soon became clear that nothing could be done to cure the disease and an appointment was made for her to see a social worker regarding alternative care arrangements.

When the social worker arrived to see Sandy she found that she was tearful and upset because the consultant had made a number of comments about needing her bed and had made her feel uncomfortable and threatened at a very vulnerable point in her life. Coupled with this, staff shortages had meant that Sandy had not been able to access the hospital chapel where she knew that she would be able to meditate in peace and quiet away from the noisy ward. She had also been unable to receive a telephone call from her family in Delhi due to a lack of telephones on the ward.

→

The social worker found Sandy a place at the local hospice. During her first week, Sandy was introduced to a range of alternative therapies including reiki and aromatherapy. She was encouraged to bring in ornaments and photograph albums from her home, and staff took a special interest in her collection of photographs from India. The hospice had a specially designated quiet area where Sandy spent many hours meditating and quietly chanting to herself.

I know that this case study is not an accurate picture of care in the National Health Service as many hospitals take very good care of their patients and offer a holistic service which meets the needs of body, mind and spirit. But the contrast between the care provided by the hospital and the hospice in our fictional account is very marked. In the hospital, Sandy's need for time, quietness and the opportunity to speak to her family are disregarded. The physical and medical care provided may have been first rate, but her spiritual needs were not met.

Service users want their spiritual needs to be recognised and taken into account

This may seem a very obvious point, particularly after reading the case study about Sandy. Thankfully, there is a growing acknowledgement, particularly in the field of mental health, that service users see their own spirituality as being of immense significance to them and as pivotal to their well-being, although this is only recognised by approximately one-third of psychologists and psychiatrists (Gilbert, 2007b).

Service users are sometimes frightened to voice their spiritual beliefs in case they are met with indifference, hostility or ridicule. Even worse, some mentally ill service users deliberately hide their religious beliefs in case they are seen as a form of delusion or illness which may lead them to be detained longer in hospital (Gilbert, 2006).

Lindridge (2007) recognises that staff may feel uncomfortable assessing a service user's spiritual needs if they do not come from the same background. Even so, this is not an excuse to disregard these needs for, as the Mental Health Foundation highlights in recent guidance, the right to freedom of thought, conscience and religion is an essential component of the Human Rights Act (Mental Health Foundation, 2007).

The influence of religion on social care

The final reason I want to suggest why spirituality is important to social work is that religion and religious values have always been closely connected with the provision of social care services. In a sense, professional social work has been built on the foundations provided by religious organisations.

As we have already established, there are clear links between religion and spirituality. Although they are not the same, they are related to one another – close cousins one might say. This relationship between religion, spirituality and social work is a large area of study and requires a separate section in its own right.

The historical role of religious organisations

Faith groups have been providing a wide range of medical, nursing and social care services to needy people for centuries. The values of compassion, service and civic responsibility that underpin all of the major religions have compelled many people of faith to commit themselves and their resources to meeting the needs of others.

In Britain, the connections between Christianity and the evolution of social care are inescapable. In medieval times hospices, which were places of rest and recuperation for travellers, were Christian institutions. The only access the poor had to any form of nursing in the seventeenth and eighteenth centuries was via Catholic nursing orders (Neuberger, 2004). Education, particularly the education of poor children, was undertaken by schools established and run by religious orders. The giving of alms (small amounts of money or food), to the impoverished was considered a Christian duty (De Swaan, 1988). It was not until the nineteenth century, however, that Christianity's involvement in the organisation and delivery of social care reached its peak.

ACTIVITY **1.3**

I wonder if you can work out what links all of the organisations listed below, apart from the fact that all of them are voluntary organisations which were founded in Britain in the nineteenth century:

- *The YMCA/YWCA*
- *The National Society for the Prevention of Cruelty to Children*
- *The Boy Scout movement*
- *Mildmay*
- *Shaftesbury Young People*
- *Spurgeon's*
- *Barnardo's*
- *NCH – the children's charity.*

Comment

All of the above voluntary organisations were founded either by individual Christians or by church groups. It has been suggested that by the middle of the nineteenth century, in London alone, there were six hundred and forty charitable organisations with a combined income of two and a half million pounds per annum (Fraser, 1976). A significant proportion of these charities were founded by Christians, as is reflected in many of their titles and mission statements:

- Sabbath Meal Society – to provide strangers with meals on the Sabbath;

- Midnight Meeting Movement – to rescue fallen women;

- Church Penitentiary Association – refuges and houses of mercy;

- Christian Union almshouses – to provide accommodation for destitute Protestants.

Other faith groups, notably the Jewish community, also provided a range of services to the destitute, poor and needy in a time characterised by significant poverty and a lack of state help.

The current role of religious organisations

While faith groups have helped to shape social work through their involvement in the evolution of care services, we should not fall into the trap of assuming that their role is purely historical. For example, all of the organisations quoted in Activity 1.3 remain important service providers to this day, although some of them have largely departed from their Christian basis.

In recent years, with encouragement from central government, hundreds of voluntary organisations have been formed to assist in the delivery of social care services. Many of these newer organisations have been created by faith groups and are entirely reliant on people of faith for funding and staffing.

CASE STUDY

Guru Ram Das project
The Guru Ram Das project in north London was created in 2003 and works with a range of people including those with substance misuse issues, homeless people, people with HIV/AIDS, older people and mental health service users. The project also visits Wormwood Scrubs prison to provide support to prisoners who have mental health problems. It has an active outreach programme and provides services to all, regardless of their faith or ethnic background.

It uses Sikh religious teachings as a foundation for its work and uses Kundalini yoga, acupuncture and meditation as a basis for holistic treatment. It relies on public donations to fund its work although it has recently received some funding from the National Lottery to expand its services.

The project is an excellent example of a contemporary charity which has developed from a religious perspective. Further information on the work and history of Guru Ram Das can be found at www.grdp.co.uk

---

The ambivalence of social work towards religion

So far I have offered an uncritical view of the significant role of religious organisations and faith groups in the history and delivery of welfare services. But not everybody in social work shares this positive view. In fact, I would argue that the relationship between social work practice and religion has often been characterised by ambivalence, even hostility.

RESEARCH SUMMARY

Canda and Furman (1999), writing from an American perspective, have traced the evolution of the connection between religion and social work. They divide the relationship into three distinct phases:

- *First phase In the nineteenth century many elements of welfare provision were provided by faith groups, particularly Jewish and Christian organisations. Non-religious humanistic approaches were also common but official, government sanctioned social work drew heavily on religious values and beliefs.*

- *Second phase From the 1920s through to the 1970s social work became increasingly professional, bureaucratic and centrally-organised. It became a job for well-educated, qualified people who were increasingly sceptical about the value of religion. Doubts about the answers provided by religion and concerns about the beliefs and actions of some faith groups, led to an increasingly secular profession.*

- *Third phase From the 1980s onwards there has been a re-emergence of interest in spirituality and more of a willingness to explore the value of spiritually-sensitive social work. This has been demonstrated by increased scholarly activity and a growing recognition that service users do have spiritual needs.*

Comment

While the analysis offered by Canda and Furman may seem a little simplistic, I would suggest that there are parallels with the development of attitudes towards religion and, by inference, spirituality in British social work.

In order to understand this relationship better, we perhaps need to spend some time thinking about why it is that religious belief has often been viewed negatively within social work.

ACTIVITY 1.4

Write down the reasons why you think that social work and social workers have viewed religion and religious belief unfavourably. As always, I would encourage you to 'think big'. Don't be afraid to put down whatever comes to your mind first, even if it does seem a little odd!

The sections below discuss my list.

The oppressive nature of some religious systems

Sometimes it is difficult to think about religion without considering the role some religious groups have had in discriminating against women, upholding patriarchy, promoting homophobia and legitimising violence and wealth. In recent years there have been a succession of scandals involving the Christian church where power has been misused by those in positions of trust and responsibility.

For example, in April 2008 on his first visit to the United States, Pope Benedict XVI, the head of the Roman Catholic Church, said that he was deeply ashamed of the activities of a number of priests who had engaged in paedophile activities or sexual abuse. One report estimates that over four thousand Catholic priests, or 4 per cent of all Catholic priests in America, have engaged in sexually abusive activity (United States Conference of Catholic Bishops, 2003). Other high-profile cases of abuse and oppression from within the Catholic community have led to a number of court cases, exposés, books and films.

The actions of religious fanatics

This is closely related to our last point, where a very small minority of people from within faith groups have sought to enforce their views and beliefs on others through violence and terrorism. This is not a new development – from the Crusades in medieval times to colonialism in the eighteenth and nineteenth centuries and to the Troubles in Northern Ireland – people have often been inspired by religion to use violence. In more recent times, the actions of Islamic fundamentalists have led to such atrocities as 9/11 and the bombing of the Underground system in London, both of which led to a heavy and tragic loss of life.

The loss of faith and the growth of secularism

Moss (2005) argues that the horrors of two world wars and the impact of such events as the Holocaust where over six million Jews and others were systematically murdered by the Nazi regime in Germany led many people to question the value of faith in the twentieth and twenty-first centuries. Simply put, God seemed absent when most needed, and was subsequently replaced by a more secular worldview. We too can echo these thoughts. One of the many challenges of faith is how people can believe in a just and loving God when there is so much poverty, hunger, starvation and injustice in the world. This question has been around as long as faith itself.

The above suggestions are not specific reasons why social workers alone would distrust religion. Most people would struggle to find much that is appealing in this negative portrayal. But there is at least one other more particular reason that we need to consider.

The knowledge base of social work

Many of you reading this book will be undertaking a social work qualification course or will be newly qualified. I imagine that what you were taught at university remains fresh in your mind. Significant elements of it will be based on traditional disciplines within the social sciences – sociology, social policy and psychology. All of these disciplines are secular and often have little sensitivity towards faith or religion. For example, the German sociologist Karl Marx, whose work has inspired and informed radical social work for many generations, described religion as being the *opium of the masses*. Other influential sociologists, such as Max Weber and Emile Durkheim, recognised the importance of religion but predicted in a modern world with enlightened views that it would become extinct. In psychology, Sigmund Freud, the father of the psychoanalytic approach, viewed religion in a number of ways – none of them complimentary. For example, religion was an illusion, a reaction to infantile helplessness or a form of paranoia.

In other subject areas, such as mental health, it is common to hear how mentally distressed people in former years were deemed to be possessed by the devil or were being punished by God for their wrongdoings.

In social policy, the role of the church in encouraging punitive legislation, designed to manage the poor and the rebellious from the Poor Law onwards, is often cited. The way the Anglican Church and the state were intertwined in past centuries leading to a domination of the educational system and an active shaping of the school curriculum is often portrayed as historically oppressive.

It is not a surprise that social workers pick up on this hostility and tend to echo what they have been taught in practice. Often on social work courses there is no teaching on spirituality and no recognition of the role of faith to provide a more balanced perspective.

Living as we do in a secular society where decreasing numbers of people attend a place of worship or profess any religious affiliation, it is uncommon to come across a health or social care worker who is entirely comfortable with religion – for the simple reason that few have an in-depth knowledge of religion, few attend a place of worship and many express a disinterest, even antipathy, towards religion. As you read earlier in this chapter, sometimes service users feel unable to raise their spiritual needs due to the embarrassed response they may receive from workers. As Baskin (2002) states in relation to social work training, the topic of spirituality is usually met with silence and the lowering of the eyes.

This diffidence, I would argue, detracts from the vibrancy and validity of social work. Our lack of spiritual understanding and our inability to harness the tools that this would bring to our practice has led to nothing less than an impoverishment of social work.

C H A P T E R   S U M M A R Y

In this chapter we have come a long way in a short time and I am aware that you have grappled with a range of ideas.

I started by introducing you to the differences between religion and spirituality and then talked about the different ideas of 'spirit'. We then began to think about spirituality and some of its characteristics:

- the ways in which it helps us to find meaning and purpose in life;

- the way it can inform and transform the way in which we view the world;

- how values and beliefs are an intrinsic part of spirituality and how both influence one another;

- how spirituality is expressed in action.

We then took a step back and thought about why we were engaging in the debate. Why is spirituality of importance to social work? If you remember, we decided that there were a number of reasons why we must acknowledge and respond to spiritual needs.

- A healthy spirituality leads to better physical and mental health.

- Science and logic sometimes do not provide a good answer to the complex problems faced by people and it can be helpful to seek spiritual solutions.

- Spirituality is important in providing a holistic, person-centred service.

- Service users want to have their spiritual needs recognised and sometimes feel that this does not happen.

We then returned to the theme of religion and looked at the influence of faith groups on the historical development of social work and how contemporary religious groups continue to play a vital part in the delivery of social care.

Finally, we looked at the ambivalence that sometimes exists between social work and religion and teased out some of the reasons why this might occur. I concluded by suggesting that this hostility has impoverished social work.

One thing I would encourage you to do at the end of each chapter is to return to the National Occupational Standards and the Subject Benchmark Statement for social work highlighted at the commencement of the chapter. You may find it helpful to review how these have been addressed within the chapter. Sometimes this is explicit, sometimes it may be less easy to discern. For example, I hope that you can see that the discussion of the ways in which religious thought has impacted on the evolution and delivery of social care enables critical reflection *about the complex social, legal, economic, political and cultural contexts in which social work practice is located* (Subject Benchmark Statement 4.7).

FURTHER READING

Holt, S (2003) *Poems of survival.* Brentwood: Chipmunkapublishing.
This is an excellent and thought-provoking collection of poetry from a survivor of the mental health system. Among other things, it talks about how spiritual need is often ignored by professional workers.

Moss, B (2005) *Religion and spirituality.* Lyme Regis: Russell House.
This was one of the first social work based books written on spirituality and remains an excellent starting point. I will be referring to the work of Bernard Moss throughout the book and the clarity he offers on what remains a contested theme.

Social Perspectives Network (SPN) (n.d.) *Research the spirit*, SPN Paper 9.
An interesting summary of a vibrant conference run by the consistently excellent SPN. Available on line at: **www.spn.org.uk**

Chapter 2

The cultural context of spirituality

A C H I E V I N G   A   S O C I A L   W O R K   D E G R E E

This chapter will help you meet the following National Occupational Standards:

Key Role 6: Demonstrate professional competence in social work practice.

- Work within the principles and values underpinning social work practice.
- Identify and assess issues, dilemmas and conflicts that might affect your practice.
- Devise strategies to deal with ethical issues, dilemmas and conflicts.
- Reflect on outcomes.

It will also introduce you to the following academic standards as set out in the Subject Benchmark Statement for social work.

4.7 Defining principles.
- Think critically about the complex social, legal, economic, political and cultural contexts in which social work practice is located.
- Acquire and apply the habits of critical reflection, self-evaluation and consultation, and make appropriate use of research in decision-making about practice and in the evaluation of outcomes.

5.1.1 Social work services, service users and carers.
- The social processes (associated with, for example, poverty, migration, unemployment, poor health, disablement, lack of education and other sources of disadvantage) that lead to marginalisation, isolation and exclusion, and their impact on the demand for social work services.
- Explanations of the links between definitional processes contributing to social differences (for example, social class, gender, ethnic differences, age, sexuality and religious belief) to the problems of inequality and differential need faced by service users.
- The nature of social work services in a diverse society (with particular reference to concepts such as prejudice, interpersonal, institutional and structural discrimination, empowerment and anti-discriminatory practices).
- The nature and validity of different definitions of, and explanations for, the characteristics and circumstances of service users and the services required by them, drawing on knowledge from research, practice experience and from service users and carers.

Introduction

In this chapter I intend to build on the work we have already done and consider the cultural context of spirituality. I want to do this in a number of ways. Firstly, I provide a generic discussion around culture and discuss how we might recognise culture and cultural influences. Unsurprisingly, I talk about the cultural context of social work and how that has changed over time. Sometimes as practitioners it feels that social work rarely moves forward or changes. Of course this is not true and there is a subtle dynamic in terms of how social work is a reflection of the society in which it operates.

I also invite you to think about the changing cultural context of spirituality in Britain. We need to be careful to note that, while I do allude to other countries, this is often a culturally specific analysis. If I were writing from a different perspective, for example discussing African spirituality, this chapter would have a very different context and flavour.

I then spend a considerable amount of time talking about men, women and spirituality. There are a number of reasons for this approach. Firstly, men, women and culture are hopelessly intertwined. Gender is heavily influenced, possibly defined, by culture and culture is influenced by gender. Secondly, as social workers we need to develop a sophisticated analysis of gender roles and the way in which formal religion and spirituality impacts on the way we perceive gender. The ways in which men and women are involved in religious observance and more secular ways of expressing spirituality continually evolve and change. As social care workers we need to have a contemporary understanding of this evolution.

Finally, I appreciate that these fluid concepts are sometimes difficult to define. After all, gender, culture and spirituality are all highly contested terms. Critical reflection, however, is a key social work skill and will help you to address the National Occupational Standards and Subject Benchmarks highlighted at the beginning of the chapter.

The importance of culture

Culture is very similar to those words that we struggled with in the introduction to Chapter 1. Words like 'care' and 'community' which on one level we all understand but find difficult to define.

Culture can be simplistically defined as the social context in which we live our lives. It refers to the language that we use, our shared perceptions and understanding of the world, our history and heritage, national institutions, our ethnicity, religion, unspoken rules such as manners and hierarchies, the way that we dress, and many other things as well. Culture is passed down from generation to generation and is given to us in a number of different ways – via our education, our upbringing in our families, the influence of our peers, and what we read and what we see in the media. Culture gives us a structure in which to operate and can be difficult for an outsider to understand or follow. Just think how difficult it can be going on holiday to a foreign country. Often the tourist can be confused by customs, practices and ways of behaving which are a mystery to them but are perfectly understandable to the local person who is from that culture.

Cultures also change over time, sometimes quite rapidly. Our changing views and ways of understanding the world help to shape the culture in which we live. For example, the way that society views gay and lesbian people is very different today from how it was twenty or thirty years ago. Those changing views have helped to shape the prevailing culture of today which makes society a more tolerant and accepting place for gay and lesbian people. Perhaps the same could be said for other minority groups. For example, people with dyslexia were previously viewed as being unintelligent and low achieving. A greater understanding of their needs has led to a changed culture in schools and wider society where appropriate support is offered for them to achieve their full potential.

I appreciate that this is a very brief and inadequate discussion of culture, but what I want you to grasp is that there is a context to what happens in life that we need to understand. Let me give you an example nearer to home which I hope will explain what I mean.

The cultural context of social work

Social work does not operate in a vacuum and needs to be understood within its cultural context. For example, in our culture we believe that it is right that children attend school, should not be over-chastised and should be adequately fed and clothed. This belief is expressed in policy and legislation and one of the pivotal tasks of social work is to ensure that children are protected and given the opportunities to thrive. In other countries and societies, however, there may be a very different cultural understanding of the role of children. In some countries, children are expected to work from a young age. In other countries heavy physical chastisement would be seen as being acceptable, even good for the child. In yet others young children are used as soldiers in a way that in this country would be found utterly unacceptable.

In our culture we also believe that older people and people with disabilities should be treated with dignity and respect, and given choices over their care. These beliefs are enshrined in legislation, particularly the National Health Service and Community Care Act 1990 which enables people to have their care needs met in their own homes. This was not always the case as vulnerable people used to be viewed very differently. For example, disabled people were viewed as being helpless, and older people were viewed as being at risk and in need of care. These widely held beliefs led to a system where people were incarcerated in large institutions, often many miles away from their families, and treated in a regimented and inhumane way. Social work had an important part to play in the old way of providing care, and of course is integral to the organisation of community care services. These very different ways of working exemplify the way that social work responds to change and provides a service which corresponds to the values and cultural beliefs of the day.

Finally, as we have already mentioned, culture is not static. It evolves, sometimes in response to changes in groups and societies. For example, in social work we are careful how we use language. In our culture the term 'client' is often used by high-status professional groups such as solicitors or accountants. The term implies a degree of dependency on behalf of the person seeking advice and reinforces the knowledge and expertise of the professional. Until recently the term client was widely used in social work. Some social workers, however, became increasingly uncomfortable with the connotations of the word and client has now been replaced by the term 'service user'. While few terms are value neutral, 'service user' at least attempts to echo the partnership values of social work and seeks to redress some of the inherent power imbalances. In other words, there has been a change in the culture of social work which is reflected in our use of language.

These are just some examples of the ways in which social work in Britain reflects the culture in which it is situated. While there will be commonalities as to how social work is understood and operates in other cultures, there will also be considerable differences.

In the same way that social work is shaped by the culture in which it exists, spirituality is also influenced by culture and, in turn, culture is profoundly influenced by spirituality.

The cultural context of spirituality

Sometimes it is difficult to decide which has the greater influence, culture or spirituality. In Western Europe and North America our culture is based on beliefs that derive from Judaism and Christianity. Our laws, our ways of understanding the world, our customs and heritage all reflect this influence. We must not, however, be too mechanistic or simplistic as there is a plurality of faiths and cultures in Britain that would not always wish to acknowledge this cultural basis. In other parts of the world where other religions or political philosophies are predominant, the culture of those countries will reflect very different beliefs and understandings.

In recent decades, however, it could be argued that the influence exerted on our culture by traditional religious belief has diminished. We undeniably live in a far more secular culture. Religious observance and attendance at places of worship has declined. Sunday is increasingly like any other day of the week and is viewed as a day when leisure, shopping and 'family time' take precedence over religious observance. Religious education in schools, which used to be exclusively Christian in content, has been replaced by a more general teaching on morals, ethics and ways of behaving which reflect a secular society. While our culture continues to reflect a specific spiritual heritage, the overall influence of Christianity continues to decline.

In a sense, this decline in Christianity has led to a gap in the market which has been filled by a diverse set of alternative beliefs and belief systems. Some echo traditionally held religious ideas while others are more secular in origin, for example the growth in the popularity of yoga, the holding of psychic fairs, shops selling healing crystals, a growing interest in traditional Chinese medicine, the acceptance of white witches and paganism, and so on. I am sure that you could think of many more examples that prove the point.

This proliferation has in turn led to changes in our culture. Our laws now offer protection to all groups of faith and belief as opposed to solely protecting Christians. Television and radio programmes now emphasise a plurality of beliefs and no longer assume a Christian stance. Official forms, such as census documents, now allow people to declare themselves to be of no religion or to name their religious background. In the 2001 census in England and Wales 390,000 people declared themselves to be followers of the fictional Jedi religion based on the popular Star Wars films. While the respondents may not have been entirely serious, this is an example of how culture and spirituality have become fused in recent years.

Culture then influences the way in which we see the world and the way that people behave and act within a particular society. It gives us a context in which to operate and on occasions we may find that context to be prescriptive and stifling. I wonder if you can remember being a small child and being invited out to tea at someone else's house. Maybe your parents insisted that you dressed in your best clothes, although you really wanted to go in your favourite pair of jeans and trainers. Maybe you had to sit at the meal table for hours, increasingly tired and bored, while the grown ups talked and talked. But cultural expectations, based on good manners and the way that children are expected to behave in public, gave both you and your parents a script to follow from which it was difficult to deviate. That, in a simplistic sense, is the power of culture. It sets the context and provides a framework for life.

Culture also has an influence on the way that adults are expected to behave. To be hopelessly stereotypical and old-fashioned, men are expected to be strong and resilient, to keep their emotions hidden and to have the role of 'breadwinner' for the family. Women on the other hand are expected to be the weaker sex, to be emotional and intuitive, and to concentrate on their role as mothers and care givers. These cultural understandings have had an effect on the way in which men and women have expressed and explored spirituality. This is a major theme, and I want us to spend the rest of this chapter looking at how women and men encounter spirituality.

Women and spirituality

The relationship between religion, spirituality and women is chequered and open to a number of different interpretations. There are often a number of stereotypes that surround women and spirituality, for example, the notion that women are naturally more spiritually aware than men due to their motherly instincts and feminine understandings. The counter-stereotype is that men, existing as they do in a world defined by work, masculinity and power, have no use for religion or spirituality and leave that area of life to women and children. Both of these understandings are flawed and require greater exploration.

What cannot be denied, however, is that women have often occupied a position of inferiority and subservience to men in all of the major world religions. For example, it was not until 1994 that the first women priests were ordained within the Church of England. The issue of female priests and female leadership continues to divide the Christian community with entrenched positions on both sides. In other religions, such as Islam, and to a lesser extent Judaism, it is rare that women occupy positions of leadership or authority.

The majority of holy texts, which guide and inspire the major religions, were written by men and present, perhaps unconsciously, a male view of the world. For example, in the New Testament, the sacred text on which Christianity is founded, St Paul advises that women should obey their husbands and take no part in church leadership. While it would be unfair not to place these statements within a specific cultural context, this message of male dominance has permeated church teaching over the generations.

Similarly, none of the major world religions were founded by women. Abraham, a pivotal figure in Judaism, Islam and Christianity, Mahavira or Vardhamana, the Great Hero who established the central beliefs of Jainism, Gautama Buddha, the founder of Buddhism, the Iranian prophet Zarathustra, the founder of the Zoroastrian faith, and the prophet Muhammad, the founder of Islam, were all male.

King (1993) has argued that women are increasingly excluded from a religion as it develops over time. In the earliest stages of development and growth, all support is required and welcomed in order for the faith to become established. Once established, however, men progressively take control and gain a monopoly of the positions of power and authority. There are some exceptions to this rule, particularly in tribal religions and where hierarchy is not of importance, for example in the Quaker movement – an inclusive nonconformist group founded in the seventeenth century which has few creeds or designated leaders.

ACTIVITY 2.1

So far in this chapter you could be forgiven for thinking that women have had no part to play in the organisation or propagation of religion. This is clearly not the case.

What I would like you to do is to think back through history and identify women who have been of importance to the major world religions. Those of you with a history or theology background might have an advantage here.

Comment

How did you get on? You may have mentioned some of the following:

- Mary, the mother of Jesus.
- Sardi Devi, Hindu guru and wife of Ramakrishna.
- Mother Teresa of Kolkata, an Albanian Roman Catholic nun.

- Fatima, the daughter of the prophet Muhammad.

- Annie Besant, the nineteenth-century leader of the Theosophical Society.

There are, of course, numerous Indian, Roman and Greek goddesses as well as female figures within mythology which could have come to mind. The female spirit or influence is very important in alternative belief systems. Let me give you an example.

In Celtic mythology the banshee, or in Irish Gaelic 'bean sídhe', is a female spirit. Some say that she is an ancestral spirit or maybe a fairy. She is able to adopt a number of different guises and appears in dark, hooded clothing as an elderly witch-like figure, a washer woman or a young girl. The banshee has a persistent mournful wail or scream and appears in the vicinity of the family home to forewarn of bad news. Hearing the banshee wail always means that a death has occurred in the family.

Belief in the banshee as a harbinger of death persists to this day in the Irish community and is a good example of how female figures are of importance in belief systems which stand outside of the world's main religious movements.

Despite having fewer positions of power than men and having had less influence in the development of faith groups, women remain crucial in maintaining the viability of many contemporary places of worship. For example, according to a study conducted by Tearfund (2007), 19 per cent of women in Britain, compared to 11 per cent of men, attend church at least once a month, and the ratio of women to men in the church congregation is 65 : 35 per cent. In many Christian churches in Britain women outnumber men and often undertake the majority of tasks within the church. In the Roman Catholic faith it is estimated that female nuns outnumber their male counterparts three to one. In Shintoism, the main religion of Japan, women act as priests and in some branches of Shinto outnumber their male counterparts. They are equally important to other aspects of Shintoism providing practical and ritual support to the (male) priesthood and acting as ceremonial dancers at the shrine. As with Christianity in Britain, without the involvement of women, Shintoism would be greatly impoverished.

The challenge of feminism

It is perhaps not surprising given the ambiguous relationship between women and established religion, that feminists have begun to question the beliefs and authority of religion. The argument goes that the major religions have been created, interpreted, led and controlled by only one sex. So how can they be universally valid for all people, especially women?

Since the 1960s there has been an increasing interest in feminist interpretations of Christianity where women writers and theologians have broken away from these traditional ways of thinking and have begun to reinterpret the core understandings and beliefs of the faith. It is outside of the scope of this book to offer anything more than a passing look at feminist theology, but I want to give you two contrasting examples of how women are seeking to redefine faith.

RESEARCH SUMMARY

Feminist theology

Ursula King (1993) argues that feminist thinking about religion and Christianity in parti-cular has a number of characteristics:

- **Change and transformation**   *Traditional understandings of faith are sexist and are partly responsible for the oppression and subordination of women in society. Feminist theology allows women to escape from these ways of thinking and permits them to explore new understandings of faith. The emphasis is not only on individual liberation, but also on the search for wider social justice in the world.*

- **Language**   *Feminist theology explores the language associated with God and chal-lenges an exclusively male interpretation of the divine. It points out, for example, that many of the titles of God in the Old Testament, a sacred text in Judaism, Islam and Christianity, are gender neutral. The feminine side of God has been neglected over the centuries and new understandings of God need to be recognised and explored.*

- **The value of experience**   *Women are suspicious of the way that experience, parti-cularly female experience, has been devalued in the church. Faith is not a rational activity and is best explored through lived experience. As an aside, there has been a growth in the use of art and creativity in the church over recent decades. Dance, art, drama and banner-making have all become commonplace as a means of exploring faith, perhaps unconsciously due to a more feminist way of thinking.*

- **Non-hierarchical and lay-led**   *The women's movement poses a number of profound questions, not least, its composition as a non-clerical lay-led movement. There is little sense of hierarchy or central authority, rather an emphasis on women coming together to explore diverse issues in a collective way. While it would be untrue to suggest that there are no ordained women or well established theologians within the movement, its loose organisation stands in contrast to the highly structured, increasingly managerial, aspects of organised religion*

I am aware that many of the examples I have used so far in this chapter are based on Christianity. It would, however, be wrong to suggest that feminist ways of thinking and interpretation are confined to the Christian faith. On the contrary, women have become increasingly visible and vocal in other faith groups. My next example comes from a different country and a different faith. I would like you to see if you can identify any commonalities between the two examples.

RESEARCH SUMMARY

Islamic feminism in Iran

The Middle Eastern country of Iran is one of the world's oldest civilisations and became an Islamic Republic in 1979 following the overthrow of the ruling Shah Mohammad Reza Pahlavi and his family. Iran has been viewed by the West as being a deeply conservative Islamic state where women are oppressed and treated as second-class citizens. While this interpretation is open to debate, there is little doubt that women in Iran have had fewer

→

rights and public presence than men. In recent years, however, female academics and those interested in the promotion of human rights in Iran have been seeking a reinterpretation of the role of women in society. Due to the religious composition of Iran this debate has taken place within the context of Islam.

Fereshteh Ahmadi (2006) has studied the growth of Islamic feminism in Iran and suggests that the movement has a number of characteristics.

- *Change and transformation   Iranian Islamic feminists have actively sought to ally themselves with movements outside of Iran, for example the Western feminist movement and the works of Western women writers. Ahmadi claims that this openness has encouraged social change within Iran, especially a decrease in conservative views about gender and distrust of the West.*

- *Language   Iranian Islamic feminists see written language as a means of control and as a way in which men have legitimised power in society. For example, feminist scholars are challenging the rule that women cannot stand for the country's Presidency which is based on one interpretation of the Koran which appears to suggest that only men can stand for such high office.*

- *The value of contemporary experience   Women in Iran have benefited from educational advances and increased employment opportunities since the revolution of 1979. As such, and with the tacit support of some progressive male theologians, women have argued that the Koran needs to be interpreted using a historical approach. In other words, it is possible to return to the original understandings of the Koran and to argue that traditional male interpretations are no longer valid in the modern world. In recent years, there has been an emphasis on women reading and interpreting the Koran for themselves.*

- *Non-hierarchical   The Islamic feminist movement in Iran operates outside of the traditional bases of power, all of which are male controlled. While there are a number of leaders, the organisation is fluid and democratic.*

I wonder if you spotted the similarities between the two examples? I would suggest that there are considerable commonalities in the struggle women have had in getting their views and voices heard in all of the established religions regardless of the culture in which they are sited. Both of the above examples show that there is an energetic engagement with religion from a feminist viewpoint. While it may be difficult to detect, it may be that over time religion will be revitalised by this engagement.

An amended faith or a new spirituality?

So far in this chapter we have concentrated on women and the more formal aspects of religion or belief. I now want us to move on and think about how women have developed new ways of expressing and experiencing their spirituality.

Feminists have posed the question whether women need to reinterpret existing religions or to create a new spiritual tradition. Both of the examples above clearly answer that question by seeking to change existing religions. Some radical feminists, however, argue that a new form of faith is required if women are to be liberated from the patriarchal oppression that underpins religion.

The Great Goddess

An example of a contemporary feminist faith is the renewed interest that has arisen over the last twenty years or so into the Great Goddess or Mother Goddess. The Great Goddess is often seen as a fertility symbol closely connected to the rhythms and seasons of the earth. It is sometimes claimed that she is associated with an ancient matriarchal age which was suppressed and superseded by the advent of male domination. In that time she was a supreme deity, the queen of Heaven, the giver of life and death.

Believers draw their inspiration from a number of different sources. Archaeology has uncovered many examples of objects which clearly depict a female goddess. Ancient religious texts, particularly Roman and Greek, support the notion of a plurality of gods, both male and female. Mythology and folklore from both East and West speak of an Earth Mother who controls the seasons and cares for the earth. Many existing religions such as Hinduism, Buddhism and the religions of the Native peoples of Africa and North America continue to reflect and revere female deities.

Views about the nature of the Goddess vary widely and she has sometimes been seen as little more than a powerful symbolic figure that unites all women across all continents and times. Others believe that she has a more tangible presence and have written catechisms and scriptures to support their faith. Some have made connections to other alternative faith groups such as white witchcraft, and there are several churches and communes dedicated to the worship of the Goddess in different parts of the world.

While recognition of the Great Goddess may be an example of a new form, or a rediscovery, of a female religion there are many more subtle ways in which women explore and express spirituality in contemporary society. Many of these expressions sit outside of the framework of conventional religion.

As has been said before, religion and spirituality are closely connected but are different. Spirituality is a much broader term and is the expression of our human spirit and unique individuality. It is the motivation within us that compels us to search for meaning and to express our identity. Within this broad definition, I want to give you a specific example of how female spirituality has been expressed which goes well beyond the framework of religion which we have used so far in this chapter.

The Greenham Common women's peace camp, 1981–2000.

Some of you may have heard or read about the peace camp which existed for nearly 19 years on the perimeter of a Royal Air Force base at Greenham Common

→

in Berkshire. The base was used to store nearly one hundred Cruise missiles – essentially flying bombs capable of carrying a nuclear payload which could hit a target hundreds of miles away. At that time there was a tense relationship between the West and the Soviet Union and both blocs were vying for military superiority. Greenham Common was an important base for the American Air Force which used it to store and test the missiles.

In 1981 a group of women marched from Cardiff to the camp to express their concern about the use of such weapons. The protesters were concerned for the safety of their children and the environmental devastation that a nuclear strike could cause. The women wanted to engage the military authorities in a debate, but this request was denied and the women decided to set up a makeshift camp in protest. Over the years, thousands of women engaged in non-violent and highly creative acts of protest against the base. For example, tactics such as building blockades, mass trespass, cutting down perimeter fencing, dancing on the missile silos, having teddy bear picnics on the base and large-scale demonstrations were all used. Many women were arrested, some were imprisoned.

Ultimately the protest was successful and in the early 1990s the missiles were returned to America and in 2000 a garden commemorating the struggle was opened on the site.

Comment

It may seem strange making a link between direct political action and spirituality. But I want you to think about the spiritual aspects of this particular protest.

Firstly, the reasons why the women were protesting was because of their concern for themselves, their children, other people and the environment. Concern and compassion are characteristics of spirituality and often force people to take action against what they perceive to be an injustice. History provides many examples of people who were compelled by their beliefs to protest against oppression or the abuse of power, for example Martin Luther King, the leader of the black civil rights movement in 1960s America, or Mahatma Gandhi, the iconic leader of anti-colonial protest in India.

Secondly, from 1982 all the protesters on site were women. In fact, Greenham Common remains the biggest female-only peace protest the world has ever seen. The way the camp was run and the way in which the protest was made created an innovative link between pacifism, feminism and environmentalism. All of these beliefs have a spiritual basis as they reflect core, unshakeable values which help define who we are as people.

Finally, there was a sense of solidarity and shared understanding among the women. The campaign could be seen as a moral crusade which gave the protesters a purpose and direction in their lives. There were elements of evangelism among the protesters as they sought to persuade others to join them. Singing, dancing, art and other forms of spiritual expression were integral to the protest. Traditional and non-traditional religious practices such as prayer wheels, chanting and yoga were also much in evidence. For many women, being at Greenham Common shaped their identity as profoundly as any religious experience.

Men and spirituality

In a sense, we have already said a lot about men in our discussion about women. We have talked about the power, even domination, which men exercise in many faith groups and have noted that men are outnumbered two to one in Christian church attendance. Earlier on in the chapter I mentioned the stereotype that men do not attend places of worship and do not have either the need or the desire to express their spirituality. As with most stereotypes, there is only an element of truth contained within it, and I want us to turn now to the rarely discussed issue of men and spirituality.

I hope by now that you will have realised that spirituality is a core element of human identity – it defines who we are as people and gives us purpose and meaning in life. This is of particular relevance to men as there has been considerable debate about male identity and purpose in recent times. In part, this is due to the decline in the traditional male roles of 'breadwinner' and head of the family. Rapid social and cultural changes have undermined our traditional understanding of who men are and what they do.

It could be argued that the place men hold in the modern world is increasingly uncertain. The demise of traditional manufacturing industries such as coal mining and steel has meant that unskilled men, who previously would have had a job for life, now find gaining any sort of meaningful employment difficult. Middle-class men (and women) need to work longer and longer hours in increasingly competitive work environments just to pay the mortgage and to maintain their standard of living.

Men are more likely than women to be physically and mentally ill, and to engage in high-risk behaviour. For example, 11 per cent of men and 4.5 per cent of women receive treatment for substance misuse. Men are six times more likely to commit suicide, and one in six men will have depression at some point in their lives, although only 20 per cent will seek treatment (Barker, 2008). Girls are outperforming boys at school and there are now more women than men at university. Women live longer than men.

CASE STUDY

Charles is a fifty-year-old Australian gay man who relinquished his Christian faith as a teenager following what he describes as a nervous breakdown where he began to question the validity and value of his life. Charles struggled with depression, an inability to make friends and social isolation all his life. As a child he found his family were emotionally distant and his father was an alcoholic. He later returned to the Catholic faith and trained to be a priest, but this did not work out and he turned to Buddhism. He finds release and a sense of peace in Buddhist techniques and is now a teacher of meditation.

Adapted from Barker (2008)

Comment

While it would be inaccurate to suggest that the majority of men live unsatisfactory, unfulfilled lives, the modern world is clearly problematical for some. For example, Charles seems to have a number of problems, doesn't he? His family background does not appear to have been helpful to him and he seems to have had real difficulty finding a meaningful place for himself in life. As a social worker you will need to develop a range of skills and insights in order to work with people like Charles. It may be that part of the problem is that he is searching for identity and security. Many of the people we work with have had such difficult experiences in life that sometimes these attributes can be very elusive. While social workers can never provide a panacea for all of life's ills, we need to recognise that the most important tool we possess is our self. If as social workers we are able to give consistency, openness, honesty and dignity to damaged people we will have at least gone some way to offering healing. It is often overlooked in the welter of paperwork and bureaucracy that accompanies contemporary social work practice that the most significant change is produced when social workers interact with service users one to one, as people to people.

Charles is perhaps a good example of someone who has left a traditional religious background and has tried to find spiritual comfort and fulfilment in a more flexible form of spirituality. Biddulph (1994) argues that men like Charles are not uncommon and that generally the main problems for men are loneliness, competition and an inability to express their emotions. In addition to this list we might also add the tendency for men to be more socially and psychologically isolated than women. All of these issues are spiritually damaging as they adversely affect identity and corrode the human spirit. Consequently, it should not surprise us that men seek spiritual solutions to these problems. We have, however, already established that men are not particularly observant. So how do men express their spirituality?

ACTIVITY **2.2**

How do you think that men express and explore their spirituality? Do you think that they do this in a different way to women? Write down your comments on a piece of paper.

Comment

Here are my thoughts.

Firstly, we need to acknowledge that despite their relative absence in some faith groups men do have spiritual needs and do express them in conventional ways. Some men do pray, read holy writings, attend a place of worship and live out their lives guided by their religious beliefs. Lippy (2005) has traced the role of men in protestant Christianity in America and concludes that men have always been present in church life and have always had a profound spirituality. This should not surprise us and merely serves to reaffirm what we already knew: that spiritual expression is common to all people.

Perhaps another way that men express their spiritual needs is through sport. Working together as a team, experiencing the highs and lows of success and failure, encouraging others and receiving support, all have clear spiritual elements. Similarly, attending sporting occasions can confirm identity and help define who we are and what we believe in. For example, the singing of national anthems before a rugby match involving any of the nations within the United Kingdom can be an inspiring sight and sound as tens of thousands of (mainly) men sing words which remind them of nationhood and reinforce their identity.

You may also have thought of the emphasis that there has been over the last few years on the image of the so called 'new man'. This view has become widespread in the media and refers to those men who are present at the birth of their children, change nappies and play with their children, take time off work to look after their children, undertake domestic chores and perhaps stay at home while their partner continues with their career. In other words, they have assumed some of those roles and identities traditionally associated with women. As with all stereotypes we need to be careful not to overestimate its significance. Government initiatives like the extension of paternity leave, the introduction of flexible working patterns and the prominence given to the importance of fathers in the lives of children have all strengthened this trend. How widespread 'new man' is in society is hard to say, but it does indicate that men are wanting to enjoy relationships and family life, explore alternatives to their traditional roles and make significant emotional attachments, all of which have clear spiritual connotations.

Social work and spiritual understanding

This chapter will provide you with a deeper understanding of culture and gender before we embark on a more detailed study of how spirituality informs the role of social work. Nonetheless, I am anxious that you begin to make connections between the themes of gender and culture and social work. I suggest that there are a number of reasons why this is important.

Firstly, many men and women that you meet in practice will define their problems in a spiritual way and may ask questions of a spiritual nature. This may not always be explicit, but a wider understanding of spirituality will help us to understand their situation.

ACTIVITY **2.3**

Imagine that you are a social worker employed by a hospice. You work with a range of people who all have either long-term conditions or are terminally ill. Consider the following vignettes and note how an understanding of culture, gender and spirituality might be useful.

- *Janet, an elderly woman is dying from cancer. She only has a few weeks of life left and*

→

wants to talk to you about the disposal of her jewellery and the continuing care of her cats. When you go to see her she begins talking about what will happen to her when she dies.

- *Yasser is the father of a young boy who has an aggressive form of leukaemia. His prognosis is not easy to predict and he is undergoing a number of invasive treatments. Yasser is often confrontational with hospice staff and seems to spend a lot of time crying and shouting.*

- *Karen is the full-time carer of an uncle who has motor neurone disease. The uncle is thinking of arranging an assisted suicide overseas. Karen opposes the idea and would value your opinion.*

Comment

At first sight, Janet seems to be a practical person who wants to talk to you about practical matters. People often attach great importance to matters that need to be addressed after they have died. They may even find it difficult to die until they are satisfied that these arrangements are in place. The jewellery may have great sentimental value to her, or may have been a significant gift or a family piece that was important to her sense of identity. Equally, the care of her cats may have given her a role in life and provided companionship and warmth. In our Western culture, older people are often not valued and it is possible that she has few connections with other people or her community.

Janet also seems to want to talk about other things. Often social workers are asked to talk about the 'big issues' of birth, life and death. If we have never thought through these issues for ourselves, it is unlikely that we will have much to say to people who pose challenging questions. Of course, social workers are allowed to have doubts and questions as much as anyone else. But we do need to have a sense of maturity and balance which comes from reflection and self-examination.

Janet's own understanding could be well worked through, perhaps based on religion, or her thoughts may be less well defined. Profound questions like this transcend gender and faith, and go to the heart of our search for identity and reassurance. They are clearly spiritual questions as they ask who am I, where did I come from and where am I going?

Yasser seems to pose a very different set of problems. On a human level we can identify with his uncertainty and distress but would find his behaviour unacceptable. It may be that there are gender issues here which need to be considered. For example, the hospice staff could be predominantly female and Yasser is misusing his masculinity. There may be cultural issues which need to be discussed. Yasser could come from a culture which is far more open to expressing high emotion and he sees nothing wrong with his behaviour. It is possible that culturally his son is of great importance as he may be the sole male heir in the family and the only means of carrying forward the family name and traditions. The son may be a much wanted only child, or maybe Yasser's wife has died leaving this son who daily reminds him of her. Some of his behaviour may relate to gender or culture, but equally he is grappling with some deep spiritual questions around potential loss, the difficulty of seeing someone in pain and the uncertainty of the future. Often people we work with, just like Yasser, have little influence over the course of their lives and feel powerless in the face of fate or structural factors. As we will consistently explore, empowering people to have an element of control, to exercise real choices and to be independent is a core function of social work.

The questions posed by Karen and her uncle are a moral minefield and would force any social worker to examine their value base. As we have discussed, values are integral to defining who we are both as people and as professional social workers and have a distinct spiritual basis. This scenario directly asks us what value do we place on life? At what point does life become worthless? Could we ever contemplate assisting someone to kill themselves? How would we feel if this was a relative, friend or service user?

In Britain assisted suicide is illegal, so assisting someone to kill themselves is a criminal offence. In recent years nearly one hundred British people have travelled to special clinics in Switzerland and elsewhere to receive assistance to commit suicide. The sight of gravely ill people having to endure hours of travel and face a death hundreds of miles away from home in the knowledge that their loved ones will have to grapple with both grief and the prospect of criminal prosecution does not sit well with many commentators. Such cases always arouse heated debate about the value of life and people's right to choose. But, as a social worker, it will only be a matter of time before you are asked to face such a dilemma, for example working in a hospital where termination of pregnancy is carried out or where elderly patients with dementia are denied life-saving interventions. These situations are never easy to resolve and often the right to choose comes at a considerable cost.

C H A P T E R S U M M A R Y

In this chapter we began by looking at the issue of culture – the social context in which we live our lives. We briefly discussed how culture and spirituality influence one another and then spent the bulk of our time exploring how women and men grapple with spirituality.

I am sure that you noticed that we spent far more time on women than men. This reflects the relative lack of research that has been undertaken on the way that men explore spirituality.

I made a number of points about women.

- I firstly suggested that the traditional religions had been predominantly organised and led by men. Women have had a major part to play in sustaining these faith groups but have often been excluded from positions of leadership and power.

- I also wanted you to note the ways in which women are increasingly adding to our understanding of spirituality. I gave two examples: one from Iran where feminists are seeking to reinterpret the holy writings of Islam, and the thoughts of Ursula King on feminist theology which is mainly related to Christianity.

- Sometimes, however, women feel so alienated from traditional religions that amending them is simply not an option. They need to find other ways of expressing their spirituality. I provided one example: the development of thinking around the Great Goddess, a historic figure who is often connected to the seasons and to fertility. You may remember that I posed the question as to whether or not this was a belief system based on a tangible entity, or whether it was merely a symbolic celebration of feminism and a recognition of the universal ties between women.

- I also suggested that women have been involved in other activities which on first sight may not appear to be linked to any notion of spirituality. I offered the example of Greenham Common where thousands of women protested against the siting of nuclear missiles in the 1980s. This direct political action had a number of spiritual components as it was based on strongly-held values and helped to define and reaffirm the identities and beliefs of many of the participants.

Throughout the chapter we did talk about men and their relationship with spirituality. In particular we discussed the threats that men have faced in recent decades with the loss of traditional roles, and established the fact that men are not especially religiously observant – although this is very different to saying that they do not have spiritual needs. We then briefly explored alternative ways in which men may seek to express their spirituality, such as the rise of the 'new man'. You may have noticed that there were some commonalities between women and men. To generalise, both seem to have difficulty expressing their spirituality in traditional ways and are increasingly turning to different, less traditional spiritualities.

Finally, we made some practical links between the issues of gender, culture and social work which I hope sets the scene for a more detailed discussion of the role of social work later in the book.

I hope that you have enjoyed this brief discussion. So far, we have concentrated almost exclusively on how individual people experience and express spirituality. In our next chapter I turn our attention to communities and argue that they too have a spiritual dimension which we need to recognise.

FURTHER READING

Ashencaen Crabtree, S, Husain, F, and Spalek, B (2008) *Islam and social work: Debating values, transforming practice.* Bristol: Policy Press.
Provides a very useful introduction to Islam and how social workers can work with the Muslim community. An essential read for all social care workers who need to be better informed about Islam and who need to hear that social work can be a value-based transformative activity.

The Journal of Feminist Theology. London: Sage; also available online (**www.fth.sagepub.com**).
A useful and accessible read for anyone interested in the lively ongoing debate regarding women and theology.

King, U (2008) *The search for spirituality: Our global quest for a spiritual life*. New York: Bluebridge.
This is a wide-ranging look at contemporary spirituality which highlights humanity's search for meaning and well-being.

Chapter 3
Communities and spirituality

A C H I E V I N G   A   S O C I A L   W O R K   D E G R E E

This chapter will help you meet the following National Occupational Standards:

Key Role 1: Prepare for, and work with individuals, families, carers, groups and communities to assess their needs and circumstances.
- Work with individuals, families, carers, groups and communities to identify, gather, analyse and understand information.
- Work with individuals, families, carers, groups and communities to enable them to analyse, identify, clarify and express their strengths, expectations and limitations.
- Work with individuals, families, carers, groups and communities to enable them to assess and make informed decisions about their needs, circumstances, risks, preferred options and resources.

Key Role 2: Plan, carry out, review and evaluate social work practice, with individuals, families, carers, groups, communities and other professionals.
- Examine with individuals, families, carers, groups, communities and others support networks which can be accessed and developed.
- Work with individuals, families, carers, groups, communities and others to initiate and sustain support networks.
- Contribute to the development and evaluation of support networks.

It will also introduce you to the following academic standards as set out in the Subject Benchmark Statement for social work:

5.1.1 Subject knowledge and understanding.
- The social processes (associated with, for example, poverty, migration, unemployment, poor health, disablement, lack of education and other sources of disadvantage) that lead to marginalisation, isolation and exclusion, and their impact on the demand for social work services.

5.1.2 The service delivery context.
- The changing demography and cultures of communities in which social workers will be practising.

5.1.4 Social work theory.
- The relevance of sociological perspectives to understanding societal and structural influences on human behaviour at individual, group and community levels.
- Knowledge and critical appraisal of relevant social research and evaluation methodologies and the evidence base for social work.

5.1.5 The nature of social work practice.
- The characteristics of practice in a range of community-based and organisational settings within statutory, voluntary and private sectors, and the factors influencing changes and developments in practice within these contexts.

5.5.3 Analysis and synthesis.
- Employ a critical understanding of human agency at the macro (societal), mezzo (organisational and community) and micro (inter- and intrapersonal) levels.

5.5.4 Intervention and evolution.
- Build and sustain purposeful relationships with people and organisations in community-based and interprofessional contexts.

Introduction

You may have realised by now that spirituality and spiritual belief is often seen in many different contrasting ways. Sometimes it is perceived as being very personal, purely a matter of individual conviction. On other occasions it is portrayed as something which characterises whole communities. Often these images are stereotypical and based on outdated, even oppressive ideas. For example the way that some communities, notably Asian people in the United Kingdom, are automatically viewed as being of the Muslim faith, or the assumption that all African-Caribbean people belong to charismatic Christian churches. In reality, there is a huge diversity of beliefs and spirituality in communities and we need to be careful not to make these assumptions.

In this chapter I want you to explore the role of social work and spirituality in community settings. As always, it is helpful to set the context for our discussion.

Throughout its history social care workers have been heavily involved in community work. It has been seen as a core task of social work to organise and promote social action on housing estates, to constructively engage with communities about their lives and problems, and to advocate with powerful bodies, like councils, on behalf of communities. During recent decades this work has been largely passed onto the voluntary sector and has been viewed by some social workers as being less important than one-to-one, statutory social work. Few social work training courses emphasise the validity of community work and even fewer social work students will have placements with community organisations. This is a matter of regret as social work should have at its heart transformation – both individual and collective transformation. The tide, however, is turning and in recent years there has been a renewed interest in how social work can again become more directly involved in community work. This change is reflected in the National Occupational Standards and Benchmark Statements for social work which repeatedly incorporate reference to communities. A casual glance at the ones I highlighted at the beginning of the chapter exemplifies this.

Horner (2003) suggests that trends within social work tend to go in circles, often prompted by short-term government and public concerns, and that themes are periodically revisited. Social work involvement in communities may be seen as one of those trends. From the outset of the profession in the nineteenth-century charitable sector to the current day, social workers have been employed to fulfil a dual function in communities: to police them and change them. Horner argues that the state has always been most interested in policing and rescuing citizens from the poorest and most deprived communities. Hence social work has been tasked to change these communities and throughout its history has been *connected to community work, to community action and indeed to political activism* (Horner, 2003, p15). Equally, we need to recognise the ongoing fragmentation of social work. Many social workers are no longer directly employed by statutory services but work within the voluntary sector. These non-statutory organisations tend to work more directly with communities and community issues than the statutory sector which often seems to be preoccupied with high-risk interventions and scenarios. Either way, there is something of a rediscovery of community as both an asset and a problem which gives even greater prominence to our discussion. It is, however, rare that we pause to consider the term 'community', or consider what makes good or poor communities. I want you to view this chapter as an opportunity to do just that.

We need to be clear that 'community' is a contested and evolving term. Sometimes we fall into the trap of over-romanticising and stereotyping the cohesion and helpfulness of communities in past generations. There may be an argument that communities were more neighbourly in past times, but equally we need to recognise that some communities were, and are, violent and threatening places. Gilbert (2003, p11) helpfully reminds us that:

> Communities can be mutually antagonistic towards each other and can also be closed as well as open and inclusive.

In other words, communities are constructed in multiple ways and are experienced in a range of different ways. Some residents will feel at home in their community while other people within the same community will feel threatened and isolated. We also need to recognise that communities are culturally defined entities. Our understanding of community will be very different to understandings in other cultures. This acknowledgement is of significance given that social workers work with a range of people who may have a very different view of community to the one that we may traditionally ascribe to. For example, some communities will seek communal solutions to social problems. I can remember some years ago discharging a frail, elderly Vietnamese woman back home from hospital. There was a reception committee of about thirty people waiting for her at home. Few of them were related to her but all were eager to help as she was venerated within the community due to her age and life experience. This example stands in contrast to the way in which some white British older people are viewed by their community and the lack of help they will receive beyond their immediate family.

In this chapter you will be exploring a range of ideas:

- the nature of community, including your own;

- what we mean by the phrases 'spiritually bankrupt' and 'spiritually healthy' communities;

- the continuing importance of rites and rituals as expressions of spirituality;

- social change and the role of social work in transforming communities;

- the place of the arts in maintaining and changing communities.

Many of the points I have made about individual spirituality are transferable to communities. For if spirituality is about our core understanding of who we are, our sense of identity and our key values and beliefs, it is reasonable to expect that larger groups of people (communities) will want to express and explore these issues as well.

Communities and globalisation

But this is immediately problematical as communities are very dynamic and diverse, and can change rapidly. Butcher, et al. (2007) refer to the complex and rapid changes experienced by some community workers as being 'white water' change, a reference to the turbulence created by a swollen river or rapids. I feel that it is appropriate to borrow this term when we think about the huge, often unplanned and unintended, changes that communities have experienced in recent years. For example, Gilbert (2007) talks about the effects of the influx of several million economic immigrants, mainly from Eastern Europe, into Britain over the last few years on a scale unsurpassed since the fall of the Roman Empire, and the impact that this has had on mental health services and the wider community – not least, we may add, the reinvigoration of the Roman Catholic Church as many new arrivals practise their religion in a more observant way than some British Catholics (Vulliamy, 2006).

This mass movement of people between and within countries is part of what we call 'globalisation'. Globalisation is often thought of in economic terms as the result of the demands of large multinational companies for flexibility and greater profit. Other characteristics of globalisation include the development of information systems, such as the internet and cheap telephone calls, and the development of transport systems which can take people long distances quickly and inexpensively (Lyons, et al., 2006).

All of these factors contribute to the fluidity of communities and, arguably, a weakening of communities as it becomes increasingly easy to maintain long-distance relationships rather than to create new friendships and connections with the people around you.

Given these pressures, you might think that it is difficult to tease out those characteristics that represent the spirituality of communities – those shared beliefs, identities and understandings that bind communities together and make them distinctive. In many ways, it is. But I want us to begin our exploration of this challenging subject by starting with something which is very familiar.

Spirituality and communities

I want you to spend a few minutes thinking about your own community. This is not as easy as it might appear, and I imagine that many of you have already begun to think about where you live as being your community. This is not wrong, but I would encourage you to consider that you may belong to a number of communities which are defined by different characteristics.

For example, a community may be based on:

- *geographical location* a village, a town, a few local streets or a university campus;

- *nationality, ethnicity or language* you may think about the growing Polish or African community in Britain, or the Welsh language community;

- *shared beliefs or interests* for example, members of the vegan community, a political party or a religious community;

- *sexuality* due to oppression and discrimination from wider society, some gay people feel most comfortable and accepted in the gay community;

- *occupation* sometimes we refer to the banking community or to the health community to describe people and organisations within the financial sector or in the National Health Service.

These are just some of the ways in which we may define community. There are many other equally valid definitions which you may have considered.

ACTIVITY 3.1

Community audit
Think about a community with which you are familiar.
Make a list of those places, people, organisations or areas within the community which you think play a part in developing the spiritual life of the community.

Comment

Some elements of communities have a clear spiritual identity and purpose, for example places of worship, faith group leaders or places of communal remembrance such as cemeteries or war memorials. Other examples that you may have thought of could be schools, places where you might find peace and quiet such as parks or woods, or leisure facilities where people can meet together. In recent years, other less obvious public places have taken on a spiritual significance. For example, it is not unusual to see memorials at the side of a road following a death in a road traffic accident which have been placed there by grieving friends or relatives as a simple act of remembrance.

There has also been a growth of interest in identifying and celebrating traditional places of worship and spiritual sites in the community. For example, in 2004 the British Broadcasting Corporation (BBC) held a competition to discover 'The nation's favourite spiritual place'. The results indicated that the public identified with a range of well-known Christian places of worship, such as the island of Iona and the Walsingham Shrine, but also chose the Avebury Ring, a site of religious ceremony which pre-dates Christianity by approximately three thousand years. For more information see www.bbc.co.uk/religion.

This interest, along with increasing numbers of articles in magazines and programmes on the radio and television, may be indicative of a growth in awareness of spirituality and a greater appreciation of the importance of the spiritual in everyday life.

Some commentators, however, offer a very different view and suggest that communities, far from being increasingly interested in spiritual expression, are devoid of spirituality and are often spiritually bankrupt places in which to live.

Spiritually bankrupt communities

In recent decades, there has been considerable debate about the nature of community and the perceived decline of traditional values and patterns of communities. While there may be some over-exaggeration of how supportive and friendly communities were in times past, many commentators have spoken about the lack of well-being and cohesion in contemporary communities.

For example, some writers have commented on the huge differences and inequalities that exist in and between some communities. The Joseph Rowntree Foundation, which produces many excellent reports on poverty and social exclusion, argues that Britain is moving back towards levels of inequality in wealth and poverty last seen more than forty years ago, with the richest sections of society becoming even wealthier and the poor becoming poorer (Dorling, et al., 2007). This disparity was exemplified by newspaper reports in June 2006 which suggested that the wives and girlfriends of the England football team had spent £57,000 in one hour on clothes and accessories in the German resort of Baden-Baden during the World Cup competition (Moodie, 2006). This contrasts with the fact that a single person under the age of 25, claiming welfare benefits will typically receive less than £50 per week.

As social workers we need to recognise the all-pervasive reality of structural oppression where well-established, powerful groups in society oppress other groups and people through the exercise of power. This leads to people being marginalised, inequality being apparent and a lack of community belonging, and legitimises the obscene discrepancies in income noted above (Thompson, 2001).

There is also considerable public and political discussion about how rising crime levels, particularly levels of violent crime, a lack of neighbourliness, poor-quality housing and education, high levels of unemployment, drugs and 'gangs of feral youths' have made some communities frightening places to live. This is not a new concern and a number of writers over the years have echoed the argument made by politicians and others that these fears about a breakdown in community stem from an erosion of traditionally held values, and problems in maintaining order and respect in rapidly changing communities (Lewis and Salem, 1986).

There are, of course, many explanations as to why these problems occur and persist. One reason that has been suggested is that contemporary communities are so fragmented and pressurised that they lack a sense of spiritual well-being.

Consedine (2002, p33) argues that many Western communities are founded on an ideology of *self-advancement, individualism, competition, and the acquisition of material goods and money.*

He argues that this unhealthy emphasis has led to a spiritual bankruptcy where communities, even whole societies, have moved away from their traditional spiritual roots and guiding beliefs and have become dislocated. This has inevitably contributed to a range of social problems such as poverty, crime and alienation.

Consedine is writing from an Aotearoa–New Zealand perspective and is particularly angry that the native people of his country, known as the Maori, have been oppressed and excluded for generations. This has led to a systematic loss of their heritage, spiritual insights and traditional practices in areas such as well-being and healing.

ACTIVITY 3.2

So far we have thought about communities in isolation and have forgotten to make the obvious point that communities are made up of individual people. In turn, communities themselves are part of a much larger entity, the nation.

Can you think of any examples where people, or groups of people, have been marginalised and oppressed by the nation where they have lived, particularly where the nation has had a distinctive religious or spiritual basis which it has used to legitimise the destruction of other forms of spiritual or personal expression?

Comment

An obvious example I thought of was the Nazi regime in Germany in the 1930s and 1940s. Nazi ideology was built on a number of different, even contradictory sources. For example, traditional Christianity, paganism and the occult were all used as tools to legitimise Nazi ideology. One particular belief was that the Aryan race, a race of white-skinned, fair-haired, blue-eyed, Germanic people would dominate the world through their natural superiority. This belief stemmed from mythology, but was supported by reference to passages from the Bible, unsound and unethical scientific research and fake archaeology. The result was that the Nazis used their beliefs to justify the murder of many millions of people who they considered were not Aryan or who simply opposed their regime. This included several million Jewish people. In the space of a few years, the religious and spiritual knowledge, heritage and expertise of the Jewish people was all but wiped out across central and eastern Europe (Thurlow, 1999).

This raises an important question. How can communities be spiritually healthy if the nation to which they belong is spiritually unhealthy or hostile to different expressions of spirituality?

Spiritually healthy communities

So how would you characterise a spiritually healthy community? This is a difficult question as it is easy to name the problems that adversely affect communities but less easy to know what we mean by 'healthy'.

Here are some of my suggestions: A spiritually healthy community is one which:

- has a distinctive character, attitude or spirit which is positive, welcoming and accepting;
- values difference and diversity;
- has a well developed sense of identity which is flexible but robust;
- recognises and responds to the strengths, weaknesses and vulnerabilities of its members;
- demonstrates commitment to its core values through action;
- promotes active citizenship and participation;
- welcomes a broad range of religious and spiritual expression.

You might not agree with my list, but I have tried to identify those aspects of communities where people are valued for who they are and are treated with respect and dignity.

Sometimes we use the analogy of the human body to describe the communities in which we live. Well-known activists or politicians are described as the 'voice' of the community. Some people may be described as the 'eyes and ears' of the community due to their local knowledge and attention to detail. Parks and gardens are described as being the 'lungs' of the community. Drawing on this analogy, I would like to suggest that the 'heart' of the community is spirituality – those aspects of the community which make it vibrant and healthy and those relationships that make it 'tick'.

Robinson (2008) simplifies this further by suggesting that the underpinning spirit, or heartbeat, of a community is demonstrated in the quality of the relationships between people within the community and through their behaviour towards one another.

RESEARCH SUMMARY

The four cornerstones
Consedine (2002, pp37–46) suggests that a spiritually healthy community is based on four cornerstones.
- **The common good** *the promotion of social conditions which enable people and groups within the community to flourish, where selfish individualism is replaced by communal solidarity and a notion that 'all are responsible for all'.*
- **Sustainability** *recognition that all communities are interdependent and that the current levels of economic prosperity for some and exploitation for others is neither ethical nor sustainable.*

→

RESEARCH SUMMARY *continued*

- *Wisdom* *individual and communal knowledge which has been gained over centuries and does not necessarily concur with rational science. This includes astuteness, discernment, judgement, foresight, sagacity, common sense and understanding. This point corresponds to some of the comments I made in Chapter 1 regarding the inadequacy of science and rationalism to answer the profound questions of life. Often a spiritual approach which draws on the well of experience is far more effective than a purely rational response.*

- *Holistic spirituality* *the need to rediscover, and to reconnect to, the spiritual roots which have given cohesion, meaning and purpose to communities over thousands of years. The search for the spirit of life which exists outside of ourselves.*

Comment

What these definitions have in common is an appreciation that all of us live in communities, that communities are important to the well-being of the individual and that spirituality has at least a part to play in helping communities to function and express themselves. How we define those spiritual aspects and the role they have is open to debate, and there is no one right answer. But as social workers involved in nurturing and supporting communities and groups of people we need to have an understanding of these spiritual dynamics.

The communal expression of spirituality: rites and rituals

As we have already discussed, spirituality manifests itself in a number of different ways and in a range of diverse places in the community. One way a community expresses spirituality is through the sharing of rites and rituals.

RESEARCH SUMMARY

The importance of ritual
Moss and Thompson (2007) remind us that shared perspectives and meanings are an integral part of life, and that many of them have spiritual significance both to individuals and to the community. Events like funerals, weddings and naming ceremonies are everyday ways of reaffirming our shared understanding of life and connections to one another.

They give the example of a Jewish funeral service where a non-Jewish person may struggle to follow the Hebrew Liturgy or to understand the symbolism behind the tearing of clothing which represents and publicly expresses grief. But on a much deeper level they will readily connect to the pain of bereavement and to the experience of loss for that trauma is common to all humanity.

It is through such shared and public activities that communities are strengthened and spirituality expressed.

Rites and rituals are important to all communities and are a way of allowing people to communally express spiritual emotions such as joy, grief and pain. They are also threads or ties which connect us to the past. After all, rituals which mark the important events of life have been around since time began.

ACTIVITY **3.3**

Make a list of all the non-religious events you can think of which could be considered to be the rites and rituals of modern society. What is their significance to the community? Do they have an openly spiritual significance?

Comment

Here is my list:

- **New Year's Eve**   a time when people get together and collectively review the past year and look forward to the coming year. These shared memories reinforce relationships and strengthen community cohesion.

- **Significant birthdays**   are often celebrated in the same way with people receiving cards and presents, throwing parties and symbolically receiving 'the key to the door'. Again, birthdays give people an opportunity to remember past times and to celebrate the joys and troubles of having strong, enduring friendships and relationships.

- **Supporting a sports team**   the passion generated by attending a sporting fixture, with its emphasis on communal solidarity, singing and a strong sense of identity, has been likened to a religious experience. There are many rites and rituals attached to sport: players and managers wearing the same 'lucky' clothes or shoes, players not shaving before a game, fans sitting in the same seats, having the same meal at every match, and the ritualised loathing for the opposition. This is neatly captured by the banner often displayed at Old Trafford, the home of Manchester United football club, which reads 'MUFC – for every Manc a religion'.

You may have thought of other examples, but a common factor is that all of these rites and rituals celebrate identity and promote relationships and shared meaning.

Spirituality and social change

Having spent some time exploring the notion of community and highlighting the spiritual nature of communities and how this spirituality may be expressed, I now want you to consider that spirituality can have a role in changing or transforming communities.

In Chapter 1 we explored the relationship between religion and spirituality and gave a number of examples of how faith groups had significantly contributed to the well-being of communities through the development of social care charities, philanthropic organisations and the wider search for social justice and reconciliation. While faith groups in Britain continue to undertake this important role, a broader understanding is required in order to appreciate how spirituality can bring about social change.

RESEARCH SUMMARY

'Secular spirituality'
Bernard Moss (2005) has been exploring the notion of secular spirituality for some years. He argues that there is a link between the belief of many faith groups in an external power, sometimes called evil or given a name such as Satan, which oppresses, misleads and corrupts people, and the social work concept of anti-oppressive practice.

Social workers recognise that the misuse of power is prevalent within society and that racism, disablism, homophobia, ageism, etc. are created and sustained by these forces, which could be seen as 'evil'.

Moss argues that social work must oppose these powerful structural forces and in anti-oppressive practice there is an underlying passionate spirituality that has an energy and a restlessness that will not find peace until truth and justice prevail (Moss, 2002, p38).

Moss goes on to compile a list of activities where social workers are involved in working with oppressed groups in an effort to transform their lives. This, he suggests, is secular spirituality at work.

Other writers, writing from a very different context, have made similar connections to those identified by Moss. For example, Cyndy Baskin, who has an Amerindian background, talks about a 'spirituality of resistance'.

RESEARCH SUMMARY

'A spirituality of resistance'
Baskin (2002) argues that in Aboriginal culture spirituality is not merely an individual system of belief but is intrinsically linked to social change and the actions required to bring about this change. For example, Native Australians believe that all life is interconnected and interrelated and that all things have a spirit. Within this belief system everybody is equal and interdependent. Consequently, when this equality is threatened and relationships harmed by the evils of oppression a spiritual response, or resistance, is required.

This takes the form of political action where oppressive social structures are challenged and oppressed people are liberated. The energy behind this action derives from the spiritual understanding of the interconnection and provides a ready link between personal spirituality and community transformation.

While there are similarities here to radical social work and conventional anti-oppressive practice, Baskin argues that these are essentially Western models which do not fully incorporate a spiritual perspective and are not sufficiently holistic in their outlook. In order for Aboriginal social work to succeed and prosper, it needs to move beyond these interpretations and develop a perspective which is firmly embedded in a culturally specific spiritual base.

These connected observations remind us that structural oppression can blight the lives of both individuals and communities through poverty and exclusion. Another related idea is that oppression can limit the spiritual fulfilment of the individual due to its detrimental effect on their self-esteem, life opportunities and well-being. (Moss and Thompson, 2007). These points are especially relevant to mental health and we will be revisiting them in Chapter 6.

The social work task; working with spirituality

As helpful as the work of Moss and Baskin is we need to be more explicit in thinking about how social work can link with spirituality to achieve change in communities.

You may remember that one of the social work Subject Benchmark Statements I highlighted at the commencement of the chapter was:

> *5.5.4 Build and sustain purposeful relationships with people and organisations in community-based contexts.*

One of the key tasks of the social worker is to assist the community to 'build and sustain purposeful relationships'. We have already stated the importance of relationships on a number of occasions and the spiritual well-being that emanates from this cohesion. A ready example of this type of activity is supplied by Butcher, et al. (2007, p81) who talk about the development of an asylum seekers' support group. This was essentially a local political organisation which sought to fight deportations and defend human rights. It drew support from a range of disparate sources – asylum seekers, existing political groups, voluntary groups, community workers and volunteers.

The task of social work in such situations is to:

• draw on the spirited response that exists within the community;

• create and develop links between different groups within the community;

• help participants to define their purpose – you may recall that having a purpose in life is a key facet of spirituality;

• assist the community to work towards social justice.

I also highlighted the next key role for you to consider throughout this chapter.

> *2.3 Work with communities to enable them to analyse, identify, clarify and express their strengths, expectations and limitations.*

We have already teased out different ideas about communities and noted that they can be spiritually healthy or spiritually bankrupt – although I would caution you to see this as a continuum and not a clear-cut distinction. Part of the task of social work is to enable communities to get to know themselves better. If you like, *to analyse, identify, clarify and express their strengths, expectations and limitations.* This is especially important in those many communities which are fractured and where competing communities live within the same geographical space. Gilbert (2003, p11) reminds us that there have been a number of riots in British cities over recent years. In the cases of Oldham and Bradford this seems to have been racially motivated. In Northern Ireland, the main motivator seems to have been religion and political aspiration.

The task of social work in such situations is to promote cohesion through dialogue and the use of safe space. Later on in this chapter I will provide you with an example of this through the pioneering work of STEER in Northern Ireland. Social work and social workers have an important role to play in bringing disparate groups together and seeking commonalities. A colleague of mine used to work in the London Borough of Tower Hamlets where there was considerable tension between African asylum seekers and the Bangladeshi community. Part of his role was to bring the groups together and help them explore their shared experiences of migration, poverty and adjustment to an unwelcoming society. This recognition led to an easing of tension between the groups.

Finally, I want us to consider the following social work Subject Benchmark Statement:

> *5.1.1 The social processes that lead to marginalisation, isolation and exclusion, and their impact on the demand for social work services.*

As social workers the fight for social justice should always define the work that we do. As highlighted by Moss (2002), the struggle for equality and justice is a spiritual quest and we need to promote change and challenge in communities. Gilbert (2003, p11), in the context of discussing the stigma and discrimination often experienced by mentally ill people in communities, notes the role of social work in changing attitudes. To borrow a phrase he employs, social work is sometimes seen as 'being in' a community, but 'not being active in' a community. In other words, social work is present but sometimes appears to work in a vacuum separated from the needs and wishes of the community.

The task of social work in such situations is as follows:

- To work with these organisations and individuals within the community who do have a vision of social justice. Sometimes these will be faith-led groups, sometimes service user-led or voluntary organisations. Often there is a spiritual well that can be drawn on in these situations and this is where local knowledge is important.

- To ensure that we lead by example. If our interventions and services are not accessible to all, free of patronising and stigmatising elements and anti-oppressive, how can we expect communities to change the way they view vulnerable people?

The role of the arts in maintaining and transforming communities

Having established a link between spirituality, oppression and the struggle for social change, we now need to spend some time thinking about how spiritual activities can bring change, even healing, to fractured communities. I am not particularly thinking about the work undertaken by formal faith groups here but about other activities which can be seen to have a spiritual basis.

For example, art is a creative process which is often undertaken in the company of other people. It can be highly satisfying to see a piece of art progress and develop over time, and can provide a sense of achievement and well-being when completed. For vulnerable or isolated people, it can be an important motivator and a reason to 'get up and go' in the morning. For all of these reasons, art is frequently seen to have a healing or therapeutic value.

ACTIVITY **3.4**

Have you ever been involved in any community, or shared, art activities? Maybe at school, or during the summer holidays? Or as part of an arts week, or to celebrate a special event in the community? Maybe you have been involved in painting a mural or creating a sculpture which is still visible in your community today.

Think back to what you did, who you did it with, and who was instrumental in leading the project.

- *How did your work help to strengthen or improve the community?*
- *Did your shared work help to build relationships and make connections between people?*
- *What benefits did you personally gain as a result of your participation?*
- *Did you feel more a part of your community after you had completed your work?*

Comment

This is not an easy task and you may have struggled to identify ways in which your work, especially if small scale, had any impact on the community or on your own sense of well-being. I can remember, however, when a community artist along with several dozen children painted a large-scale mural on the gable end of a town house in my home town. One of the children, who is now well into her twenties, still recalls with considerable pleasure that she painted the ducks! In a sense, it stands as a very visual reminder of her childhood and brightens up that part of the town.

In recent years there has been an increased interest in the use of art and other creative activities such as dance, drama, singing and music as a means of improving the lives of individuals and the well-being of communities.

Here are just some of the ways in which they can be therapeutic:

- *as a way of developing creativity and expression;*
- *helping people recover from mental illness;*
- *promoting relationships and connections in the community;*
- *encouraging people to lead a healthier lifestyle by keeping fit, getting out of their homes more, meeting different people, etc.;*
- *by improving people's self-esteem;*

- *reducing health and social inequality;*
- *as a way of improving the local environment.*

(Heenan, 2006)

I now want you to consider two examples of artistic projects which have promoted individual growth and have had an impact on the community.

RESEARCH SUMMARY

The STEER 'art as therapy' programme

STEER is a community-based voluntary organisation in Northern Ireland. It was established in 1998 by service users and carers all of whom have had some experience of mental illness. STEER is an acronym and stands for Support, Training, Education, Employment and Research.

Northern Ireland has one of the highest levels of social and health deprivation in the United Kingdom. Many of its communities have been traumatised due to years of on-going sectarian violence and conflict, known locally as 'The Troubles'. The days of inter-communal violence are, at the time of writing, thankfully past, but the mental and physical scars and divisions caused by the conflict still remain.

STEER runs a number of projects to help people recover from mental illness and the discrimination and stigma that are often attached to being mentally distressed. As part of their supported recovery programme, service users can choose to take part in an 'art as therapy' module which lasts for ten hours a week over a ten-week period. There is no charge to the service user and the emphasis of the programme is not so much on the quality of the work produced but on the therapeutic value of producing it.

The art as therapy project was evaluated to discover what benefits people could identify from their participation.

Three broad themes emerged from the research:

- ***An improvement in confidence and self-esteem*** *A number of people interviewed reported that their overall level of confidence had improved as a result of attending the project and that they felt more able to address the issues that had led them to become mentally ill.*

- ***A feeling of safety*** *Living in communities which have had long experience of conflict and violence, many people were understandably reluctant to disclose personal information or to engage with strangers because of the possible repercussions. The art project was described as being a safe place, where people could be themselves away from the pressures of the outside world and the limitations of statutory mental health provision.*

- ***Empowerment*** *Participants felt that membership of the group had given them acceptance, a feeling of inclusion and a sense of equality all of which had enabled them to experience a feeling of liberation. Some reported that they felt positive about themselves for the first time in years, while others used the project as a springboard to go on to other courses or voluntary work.*

(Heenan, 2006)

Comment

You may feel that Heenan's research tells us a great deal about the value of art therapy for individual people but are a little puzzled as to how this relates to our theme of community transformation.

What I would like you to consider is that healthier people make for healthier communities, and in particular that the STEER project produced the following subtle changes in the communities from which the people came.

- Participants reported that they felt 'safer' and that the project offered them a safe space in which to work, communicate and relate with other people. As participants interacted and shared their common experiences, barriers were being reduced and tensions eased. This must have transferred into the community and helped, albeit in a small way, to heal the historic divisions caused by 'The Troubles'.

- Participation in the project enabled people to become more active citizens in the community – volunteering, finding employment, going on courses. This increased involvement must have enriched the life of the community and given it more vitality and energy.

- Participation in the project helped to mitigate against social exclusion. People felt more confident about themselves and their lives and had a greater sense of being valued and included for who they were as people. Given that people with mental health problems are often excluded from the opportunities and rewards of society and that the project was situated in a very damaged community, these positive feelings must have generated a wider beneficial effect.

I want us to explore another art form now, music, which is often seen as having a spiritual dimension. Music can often 'lift us out of ourselves', or influence our emotions making us feel happy or sad, or evoke memories of past events and relationships. It has been used as a way of heightening spiritual and religious feelings for thousands of years and is an important relaxation for many people.

ACTIVITY 3.5

Is music an important part of your life?
Make a list of the ways in which music is significant to you – this may simply be listening to the radio or singing in the shower!
What psychological or social benefits do you think you gain from your enjoyment of music?

Comment

Music is and always has been an integral part of culture and often provides the backcloth to the most important events in life. It can be seen as the accompaniment to a range of significant life activities from the cradle to the grave, through lullabies, games and dances and work songs, as battle music, and at ceremonies and rituals for life events such as coming of age, weddings and funerals (Gregory, 1997).

Many studies have shown that singing is good for you and has a number of positive effects on psychological, physical and emotional well-being (Stacy et al., 2002; Hillman, 2002).

But involvement in music is rarely a solitary, individual activity. Orchestras, bands and groups play together, while concert goers listen together and often show their approval, or disapproval, in unison. Interest in music leads to discussion with other people in conversation, on the internet, in music magazines or through fan clubs. Being a member of a choir or learning a musical instrument is often seen as an enjoyable leisure pastime to be shared with others. Religious faith groups have used voice and music for thousands of years as a shared, communal activity which assists the congregation to worship.

Given the communal nature of music, it is worth exploring if this art form could have a positive impact on communities.

RESEARCH SUMMARY

'Call that singing?'

In 1989 Sue Hillman established a community arts project entitled 'Call that singing?' to celebrate the city of Glasgow's time as European capital of culture. The project was so successful that it ran for many years beyond its anticipated lifespan.

'Call that singing?' encourages people of all ages and abilities to participate in mass choirs. Rehearsals are light hearted and membership of the choir is entirely voluntary with no subscription or auditions. Public performances take place in a number of venues, many of them non-traditional venues for music, and are well supported and received.

In 2000 research was undertaken to evaluate the impact the project had had on older participants. Older choir members who were part of the evaluation indicated that their lives had been improved in a number of ways. For example, their physical health and emotional well-being had improved, their confidence and understanding of singing had increased, and they felt that their overall quality of life was better for being involved in the project.

(Hillman, 2002)

CASE STUDY

Margaret is a 45-year-old woman with minimal learning difficulties who lives alone in a one-bedroomed flat in a tower block. She finds her community a hostile place in which to live and is particularly frightened to go out at night or to leave her flat in the morning when there are schoolchildren about.

Margaret has recently begun attending a reading group at the local library where stories are read and free refreshments are available. Through her attendance at the group

→

CASE STUDY *continued*

Margaret has made several new friends and acquaintances, become interested in taking books out of the library and has signed up for an introductory computer course. Some other members of the group live within walking distance of her flat and they have agreed to informally meet every week to talk about the books they are reading.

As a result, Margaret feels happier in her community and is able to go out more than she did.

Comment

As a social worker you will come across many people like Margaret. Her needs are not particularly high and she may not qualify for formal statutory social work assistance. Nonetheless, she is a vulnerable woman whose quality of life could quickly deteriorate to the point where more formal support is required. As a social worker you need to develop an in-depth knowledge of what is available in the community to assist people like Margaret. You will often act as a 'signpost' for people pointing them to groups and organisations where their needs can be met. This local knowledge should not be underestimated as it can take years to acquire and provide you with many valuable contacts.

As we have previously noted, increasing numbers of qualified social workers are now employed outside of the statutory sector and undertake a pivotal role in assisting people like Margaret and through sustaining community work. Social care staff formally employed in community projects, and of course the army of unpaid volunteers who assist them, could be seen as the glue that binds fractured communities together. Without their input communities would be much poorer places in which to live. This notion of adhesion and communality neatly brings us to our next point.

Social capital

What I would like you to consider now is that both of the research examples we have discussed, and our previous thinking about rites and rituals, have increased the 'social capital' of the participants, which in turn has had a positive impact on their communities.

The concept of social capital has a long history and has become a widely used idea in areas such as education, politics and sociology. Social capital refers to those social networks (relationships, friendships and connections) that provide us with support and enhance the quality of our lives. Social capital encourages trust between people and reciprocity where ideas, friendships and resources are mutually shared and exchanged. It is often thought of as the 'social glue' that binds us together and enables us to feel part of the community (Bourdieu, 1977; Putnam, 2001; Lyons, et al., 2006).

Earlier in this chapter we reiterated that spirituality is about our core understanding of who we are, our sense of identity and our key values. All of these aspects are enhanced or influenced by the relationships that we have and the benefits that derive from knowing other people.

Projects, like STEER and 'Call that singing?' then are spiritual in two different ways: firstly, through the creative activity itself – this encourages people to explore new ways of expressing themselves and to learn new skills, which in turn, produces something of value; and secondly, the connections and feelings of community that are created which increases the social capital of participants. Both of these benefit the wider community in subtle but tangible ways.

C H A P T E R S U M M A R Y

In this chapter you have begun to look at the connections between spirituality and community. We examined the problematic nature of communities and noted that they are open to constant change and movement. This sometimes makes it difficult to determine what we mean by spiritually healthy or spiritually damaged communities, although we did some thinking about what these two ideas meant.

You then looked at ways in which communities might express spirituality. Rites and rituals are important here. Using the social work Subject Benchmark Statements and Key Roles as a broad guide, we then spent some time trying to tease out the role of social work.

We then used two examples of art projects to make the following points:

• Art is often a communal activity which is shared with other people.

• The creative process itself, which often takes the person 'out of themselves', is an expression of spirituality.

• The benefits gained through participation are of benefit to both the individual and the community.

• In particular, there is an increase in 'social capital' which results in a greater sense of support and inclusion.

FURTHER READING

Bornat, J, et al. (1997) *Community care: A reader*. Basingstoke: Macmillan.
While this book is now somewhat dated, it still provides a comprehensive overview of many pertinent issues relating to community and care. Section one provides an accessible and comprehensive discussion of the nature of community and looks at such interesting issues as the contested meaning of community, the role of neighbours and the role of women.

Davies, A (2008) *The gangs of Manchester: The story of the Scuttlers, Britain's first youth cult*. Wrea Green: Milo Books.
Milo Books are independent publishers who have produced a number of books analysing the history of communal violence. This book offers an insight into nineteenth-century gang warfare in a heavily industrialised and poverty-stricken setting. It serves to remind both policy-makers and social workers that fractured and hostile communities have been around for many years.

Horner, N (2009) *What Is social work? Context and perspectives*, 3rd edition. Exeter: Learning Matters.
Chapter 2, 'The beginning of social work: the comfort of strangers', offers an interesting and accessible introduction to the evolution of social work and the *raison d'être* for community involvement.

Nash, M, and Stewart, B (2002) *Spirituality and social care*. London: Jessica Kingsley.
This is a well regarded and interesting anthology of writings which emphasises the importance of community.

Currents: New Scholarship in the Human Services.
The *Currents* journal is a peer reviewed academic journal freely available from the University of Calgary Press at: **www.ucalgary.ca/currents/**. I have found many interesting articles on spirituality in their back catalogue. In particular, it usefully showcases non-Western articles such as the one written by Cyndy Baskin referred to in this chapter.

Chapter 4
Working with spirituality: Older people

A C H I E V I N G   A   S O C I A L   W O R K   D E G R E E

This chapter will help you meet the following National Occupational Standards:

Key Role 1: Prepare for, and work with, individuals, families, carers, groups and communities to assess their needs and circumstances.

- Work with individuals, families, carers, groups and communities to identify, gather, analyse and understand information.
- Work with individuals, families, carers, groups and communities to enable them to analyse, identify, clarify and express their strengths, expectations and limitations.
- Work with individuals, families, carers, groups and communities to enable them to assess and make informed decisions about their needs, circumstances, risks, preferred options and resources.

It will also introduce you to the following academic standards as set out in the Subject Benchmark Statement for social work:

5.1.1 Social work services, service users and their carers.

- The social processes (associated with, for example, poverty, migration, unemployment, poor health, disablement, lack of education and other sources of disadvantage) that lead to marginalisation, isolation and exclusion, and their impact on the demand for social work services.
- Explanations of the links between definitional processes contributing to social differences (for example, social class, gender, ethnic differences, age, sexuality and religious belief) to the problems of inequality and differential need faced by service users.
- The nature of social work services in a diverse society (with particular reference to concepts such as prejudice, interpersonal, institutional and structural discrimination, empowerment and anti-discriminatory practices).

5.1.4 Social work theory.

- The relevance of sociological perspectives to understanding societal and structural influences on human behaviour at individual, group and community levels.
- The relevance of psychological, physical and physiological perspectives to understanding personal and social development and functioning.
- Models and methods of assessment, including factors underpinning the selection and testing of relevant information, the nature of professional judgement and the processes of risk assessment and decision-making.

5.1.5 The nature of social work practice.
- the nature and characteristics of skills associated with effective practice, both direct and indirect, with a range of service users and in a variety of settings.
- the processes that facilitate and support service user choice and independence.

Introduction

Having spent the first part of the book exploring some of the complexities of spirituality, I now want us to turn our thoughts to social work practice. In subsequent chapters I will focus on one particular area of social work intervention and offer some thoughts as to how spirituality and spiritual understanding needs to be an integral part of the work that we do.

In this chapter, I want us to concentrate on working with older people. There are two reasons for this. Firstly, spirituality within adult care is unevenly developed. Considerable work has been undertaken on spirituality and mental health, and also within the arena of palliative care. Much less has been said about spirituality and disability, or how we might engage with vulnerable people who do not fit into any organisational box but still have needs which must be addressed. Given this unevenness of approach, even lack of interest, I hope in a small way to begin to redress the balance. Secondly, talking about older people gives us an opportunity to discuss general issues which are relevant to all people but may have particular significance for those who are older, for example issues around loss and memory impairment.

Ageing and spirituality

Firstly, we need to acknowledge that spiritual needs do not necessarily change in older age. All people regardless of their age need to have meaning and purpose in life, a sense of self and identity, and the opportunity to enjoy relationships. But in older age these needs are influenced, perhaps extenuated, by experiences common to the ageing process. For example, the presence of loss, an increasing awareness of the closeness of death and a commonsensical understanding that there is less life ahead than there was before!

In order to frame our thinking about spirituality in older age, I want us to consider what two authors have said about the spiritual needs of older people.

The spiritual tasks of ageing

The first model which captures some of the spiritual issues of older age has been developed by MacKinlay (2004) in her work concerning the spiritual tasks of ageing. You may be familiar with similar models as many theorists of human development, such as Havighurst and Erikson, have produced sequential models which seek to explain some of the phases or tasks that people need to accomplish if they are to successfully move from one stage of life to the next.

This model, however, is different as MacKinlay suggests that these *spiritual tasks* are not jobs or phases to be completed before one dies but are part of a psychological/spiritual process which assist the person to make sense of their life and find meaning to some of life's dilemmas. They do not occur in any set order but are interrelated and may be revisited or revised by the older person on a number of occasions.

The first task is to find *intimacy and relationships*. Writing from a faith perspective, MacKinlay suggests that this could be with God, but equally it may be the search for rewarding relationships with other people. All of us need to be known and respected for who we are, regardless of our imperfections and limitations. A significant part of our humanity is the need to be in relationships with one another. All of us need to have people with whom we can discuss our hopes and problems. This, however, can be problematical for some older people as they may have lost their partners and friends, live alone or be estranged from their families. As we suggested in the previous chapter, communities can sometimes be unsupportive places to live where it is diffi-cult to forge and sustain relationships, particularly if you are unable to actively participate in the community.

Connected with this task is the search for *hope*. Hope is essential to life and is one of the crucial ingredients of what we might describe as well-being, a shorthand term for happiness and contentment with life. As MacKinlay (2004, p82) comments:

The human spirit is nourished by and flourishes on hope.

What we hope for can be as varied as who we are, for example the hope that we might enjoy better times, the hope that we will have good health, the hope that we will see our loved ones more, the hope that we will be released from pain. MacKinlay adds to this list by suggesting that hope in older age is often associated with the tangible desire to see children and grandchildren well established in their lives. Ulti-mately, all of us need something to motivate us, to give life purpose, something to live for. A very different emotion to hope is fear. While we need to be careful not to be either ageist or to make assumptions about the quality of life in older age, many people view and experience old age as a time of fear and anxiety, for example the fear of death or a close bereavement, fear of losing a home, fear of losing one's memory, the fear of poverty, and so on.

Another spiritual task is to *transcend loss or disability*. One of the real fears of older people is that they will lose their independence and become reliant on others, some-times complete strangers. MacKinlay argues that there is a great emphasis in the Western world on being and remaining independent, while in fact throughout our lives all of us are reliant on other people and other people rely on us – we are by nature interdependent. One of the challenges of older age is to work through, or transcend, the experience of loss, to be comfortable with becoming more reliant on others, while still retaining the individuality that makes us who we are.

The concluding spiritual task is to *find final meaning*. This is where life is reviewed and reconsidered. Often it is difficult to make sense of some of our experiences, particu-larly if unwelcome or hurtful. Older age gives us the opportunity to:

. . . go back over life and affirm, reframe, to see who we really are in the light of all that we have been and have experienced and learned throughout our lives.

(MacKinlay, 2004, p80)

As you can see, there is a sense of finality and successful completion here. You may feel that these tasks are overly optimistic and dependent on the person having both the mental capacity and an ability to be self-reflective. Equally, you may know people who, as the famous poem by Dylan Thomas records, have not *gone gently into that good night, but have raged against the dying of the light* (Thomas, 2000, p148). For some, older age will be an unsatisfactory and painful finale.

Affirmation, celebration, confirmation

Jewell (2004) adds to this list of tasks by drawing our attention to a number of other spiritual needs. He suggests that some older people feel that their lives no longer have purpose. They have retired from work, have raised their families and may have withdrawn from hobbies or commitments which previously gave their lives purpose and direction. The voice and views of older people in wider society often go unheard, and there is a danger that they become invisible and seen in negative, stereotypical ways. What is required is *affirmation* – the collective and individual restatement that their lives are both valued and valuable.

Coupled to this is the need for *celebration*. All of us need to celebrate our achievements and accomplishments, for these help to reinforce who we are and our self-worth. Older people often have milestones such as notable birthdays and anniversaries to celebrate, but sometimes no one to celebrate with.

Finally, Jewell talks about *confirmation*. In many ways this relates back to my comments at the end of the last section. Increasing frailty, vulnerability and thoughts about death often raise fundamental questions and doubts in people's minds. For example, is this all there is to life? Or, has my life been worthwhile? What is required is confirmation, confirmation that those core beliefs and values which have sustained and guided throughout life are as meaningful now as they were in times past.

Sometimes those core beliefs can be difficult to access for someone whose memory is impaired. Robert Davis, a Christian minister from America, wrote about his experience of having Alzheimer's in the 1980s. He records that the first loss he had to endure was the inability to reach those comforting memories which had sustained and guided him over many years. He found it increasingly difficult to pray, and his sense of faith seemed to decrease as his impairment gathered pace (Davis, 1989).

All of these spiritual tasks or needs are interconnected. For example, if you do not enjoy intimacy and good positive relationships it is unlikely that your life and life events will be celebrated. Equally, if affirmation is absent, if there is no acknowledgement that your life has been worthwhile, it could impact on your ability to find meaning in older age. What struck me is that many of these characteristics relate to the way that older people are valued and how important spiritual aspects are to having a positive experience of older age. I want us to return to these tasks later on in the chapter and use them as an aid to analysing a case scenario.

I now want to turn your attention to older age and dementia, and use the experience of dementia as a way of exploring spirituality. Those of you who work in adult care services will know that a significant part of your work will be with older people who have been diagnosed as having a memory impairment caused by a dementing process. We need to be clear, however, that the majority of older people do not have dementia, and memory impairment is not solely an issue for older people.

Spirituality and memory loss

According to the Alzheimer's Society, there are currently 700,000 people in the United Kingdom with dementia, with this figure expected to rise to over one million by 2025 (www.alzheimers.org.uk).

RESEARCH SUMMARY

What is dementia?

Dementia is an umbrella term used to describe a range of illnesses or syndromes – there are over one hundred different types of dementia. Alzheimer's (disease) is the most common form of dementia and the most widely known. It is a progressive disease where protein develops in the brain causing a loss of brain cells. It is irreversible and is characterised by a number of symptoms including memory and language impairment, disorientation (not knowing where you are in time or place) and changes in personality and behaviour, for example increasing aggression or sexual disinhibition.

One of the common features of dementia is memory impairment, often an inability to remember in the short term. Conversely, there is some evidence to suggest that the long-term memory is actually boosted by dementia. It is not unusual for someone to be able to clearly remember events from past years but be unable to recall a conversation they had a few moments ago. Approximately one person in twenty has memory impairment in the seventy to eighty age range. This rises sharply with advancing age with one person in five having dementia in the eighty plus age bracket, and one in three for people over ninety (Crawford and Walker, 2005, p72).

It is unclear what causes dementia. Over the years many suggestions have been made including the use of aluminium saucepans, genetic factors, smoking, head injury and high blood pressure. There are a range of treatments available, notably medication, but these only alleviate the symptoms and slow down the progress of the disease rather than provide a cure.

For further information see: www.alzheimers.org.uk.

The loss of personhood

Older people can be viewed negatively and portrayed as being a burden and of little value to society. This is particularly true for people with dementia who are often viewed as being helpless or childlike. For many years there was a prevailing view that dementia was almost a living death. This was even articulated by a past president of the Alzheimer's Society, Jonathan Miller, who described someone with the condition *as an uncollected corpse that the undertaker cruelly forgot to take away* (Miller, 1990). While the remorseless nature of Alzheimer's needs to be acknowledged we must be careful not to fall into the trap of seeing people with dementia as without full human value or worth. Eileen Shamy (2003), a writer from Aotearoa/New Zealand, suggests that the emphasis placed on usefulness, progress and profit by the pioneering spirit of her nation makes people with memory loss almost invisible. Much the same could be said about other Western societies where profit, work and an emphasis on youth and beauty mean that older people, especially those with limitations, are often ignored.

The writer who has probably done most to address the devaluing and exclusion of people with cognitive impairment is Tom Kitwood. Professor Kitwood came from a psychology background and wrote extensively on dementia until his untimely death in 1998. He originally trained for the priesthood but in later life renounced his attachment to religious faith but retained his keen interest in spirituality. Kitwood argued that theology, philosophy and secular ethics all emphasise that people have *absolute value.* Building on these foundations, he argued that everyone should be treated with respect and valued for who they are regardless of whether they have insight, rationality or memory. Over time he developed the concept of *personhood.* That is...*a standing or status that is bestowed upon one human being by others, in the context of relationship and social being. It implies recognition, respect and trust* (Kitwood, 1997, p8).

I hope that this section on dementia has at least raised your awareness of some of the issues and given you an insight into how some writers have tried to move away from a medical/clinical understanding of memory loss in older age towards a much more human understanding. There is a profound spiritual emphasis within the work of both Shamy and Kitwood. Both confidently emphasise the explicit value of the human spirit – that core of humanity which cannot be destroyed by either impairment or by the disabling views of society. They also remind us that memory loss needs to be considered within its social and cultural setting.

As social workers we need to be mindful of the social context of a situation and take into account the sociological factors that influence our understanding. This is highlighted by one of the Subject Benchmark Standards that I invited you to consider at the beginning of the chapter. Standard 5.1.4 reminds us that we need to take into account:

> *the relevance of sociological perspectives to understanding societal and structural influences on human behaviour at individual, group and community levels.*

The writers we have studied so far offer a number of sociological insights: the way society views age and ageing, the cultural emphasis on independence and the way in which older people are expected to manage older age. This theme is evident throughout the book and I hope that you periodically pause to reflect on the social context of social work and spirituality.

What I would like you to do now is to consider the case study below and begin to make some links with spirituality and good spiritual care. The case study will develop incrementally as I want us to spend some time thinking about the issues that could arise for a social worker involved in the case.

CASE STUDY

Mrs Hardy
Mrs Hardy is an 84-year-old widow who lives alone in an owner-occupied bungalow in a suburb of a small town. The bungalow was bought following the retirement of her husband some twenty years ago. Mrs Hardy has one daughter and three grandchildren who live some distance away and rarely visit. They have very busy professional lives, and while not uncaring towards Mrs Hardy, have little time to give to her. Since Mr Hardy died twelve months ago, the family have only visited three times and do not initiate contact. Mrs Hardy rarely goes out and seems to have no friends.

Since the death of her husband, Mrs Hardy seems to be quite confused. Over the last few months she has burnt out several pans, has been found wandering aimlessly in the street by neighbours and has telephoned her daughter in the middle of the night on several occasions saying that her husband is missing.

A referral has been made to the local adult care team requesting an assessment. The team manager feels that the most appropriate professional to complete the assessment is a social worker and the case has been allocated to you.

You visit Mrs Hardy for the first time. She is sitting on the settee with her daughter and appears anxious and upset. Her daughter is already saying that she has to leave in half an hour and that her mother should be in a home.

At first glance this is a typical scenario for any adult care social worker. It would seem appropriate that an assessment of need is undertaken using the framework of assessment and care management provided by the National Health Service and Community Care Act 1990. This would involve the completion of assessment documentation and decisions being made regarding eligibility and service provision. In other words, the social worker would be required to engage in a process-driven bureaucratic task. There is a risk that the case will be opened, reviewed and closed in a matter of weeks with little regard to the emotional or spiritual needs of Mrs Hardy. Her care needs may well be addressed and the quality of her life improved, but her humanity will take second place to the administrative needs of contemporary social care.

What I would encourage you to consider is that this situation is in effect a spiritual crisis. Of course there are health and social care issues related to the onset of dementia and physical frailty but these are contributing factors to the spiritual crisis that is surrounding her. One of the principal spiritual problems that she is experiencing is an absence of *intimacy and relationship.* Her husband has died, her family are largely absent from her life, she rarely sees anybody from the local community and she has no friends. Consequently, there are few opportunities for her to experience, in the words of Jewell, *affirmation, celebration and confirmation* as these spiritual needs can only be met via interaction with others.

There are other spiritual elements to the crisis that we also need to consider. For example, I wonder if Mrs Hardy has meaning and purpose in her life? As we explored in Chapter 1, to have meaning and purpose is a core spiritual need for this helps to shape our identity, our understanding of who we are and why we are here. Often meaning and purpose derive from having a substantive role in life, like a job or task. Many older people lead active lives and have an important role in raising their grand-children, doing voluntary work or taking part in leisure activities. There is no indication that Mrs Hardy enjoys any of these life affirming roles.

It would also appear that Mrs Hardy's life is characterised by loss. She has lost her husband, she is beginning to lose her memory and she is potentially losing her inde-pendence. It is likely that over the next months and years her experience of loss will increase and deepen. Consequently, an ongoing element of the crisis is, and will be, her struggle to *transcend loss.* An ageist assumption is that older people cope better with loss than younger people. This is not necessarily the case and Mrs Hardy's life will be diminished as much as that of a younger person by her cumulative experience of loss.

Having established that there are a number of spiritual dimensions to this crisis, I want us to turn now to the skills and insights required to meet these needs.

Building relationships

Firstly, I want you to consider your purpose in engaging with Mrs Hardy. It may well be that you have been tasked to decide if the situation merits further intervention or to complete an assessment of her needs. Whatever the stated reason, I would suggest that you are there to build a relationship.

> *Remember your purpose – relationship building. Doctors and social workers and others whose work necessitates an emphasis on information-seeking, rather than relationship building communication, have sometimes concluded that, because it is extremely difficult to obtain information from people with dementia, all communication is therefore too difficult to warrant the effort.*

(Shamy, 2003, p71)

This is an important point. It is far too easy to focus on the process and forget that there is a person at the heart of your intervention. I often feel that service users get lost in a welter of forms, processes and procedures in contemporary social work practice. There are so many targets and outcomes to meet, so many cases to be processed and so much paperwork to be filled in, it is little wonder that social workers are in such a hurry to get the job done! And yet, the responsibility and privilege of social work is that it is built on relationships. As Warren (2007) points out, the building of a relationship with a service user is crucial to the success of the social work task. If social workers do not take time to engage with those they are working with, listen to their needs and respect their views, meaningful service user participation will not take place. If we are to build a relationship with Mrs Hardy at this initial stage we need to take time to listen and respond.

The importance of communication

ACTIVITY 4.1

I want you to imagine that you are the social worker who is sitting with Mrs Hardy who, if you remember, is anxious and upset. What are the key ways in which you will communicate with her?

Comment

You may have noted some of the following points:

- Introduce yourself and say why you are there and what you will be doing.

- Be clear, do not rush.

- Repeat information if necessary.

- Be prepared to provide written information or to write things down.

- Acknowledge the presence and importance of the daughter but concentrate on Mrs Hardy.

- Use interpersonal, non-verbal skills and remember to make eye contact.

Active listening and responding to the expressed needs and wishes of the person is at the core of good communication and is a vital skill for anyone employed in the caring professions. If you cannot communicate well in a number of different settings with a diverse range of people, it is unlikely that you will be a good social worker. All of the characteristics we noted help to strengthen the *personhood* of Mrs Hardy by showing respect for her as a person and valuing her for who she is.

I want us to briefly return to Kitwood for a moment and consider a concept which is related to his work on *personhood*. The concept of *malignant social psychology* derives from his research into traditional forms of residential care for older people with dementia and describes the depersonalising aspects of care which he frequently encountered. I am not going to review all of the characteristics of *malignant social psychology* but will concentrate on those which speak about communication and will relate them to our case scenario. In many ways, the following characteristics provide a list of the ways in which we should not communicate with Mrs Hardy.

- *Infantilisation* treating her as if she were a child without the capacity or the ability to make judgements.

- *Labelling* seeing her purely as someone who is confused or demented and using that label as a basis for our interaction. Labels can on occasions be helpful and often are the key to accessing resources in adult care. For example, in order to access significant resources in the community care assessment process we label people as being in the 'critical' band of eligibility. But often these labels deny *personhood* and are the enemy of holistic assessment as they confine people to convenient boxes and groups and deny individuality.

- *Outpacing* talking too quickly, giving options and information at a pace that Mrs Hardy cannot follow. Often we forget how complex the information is that we use. People in crisis who have never had any contact with health or social care professionals before can easily become confused by the welter of information, leaflets, contact cards, etc. that we need give to them. Often we rush people to make profound decisions about their homes and their futures in a way which is dehumanising.

- *Invalidation* failure to engage with the person and acknowledge the reality of their experience. This, for example, could be a failure to recognise the anxiety and distress of Mrs Hardy. Equally it could be that we forget that Mrs Hardy is the expert on her own life. She will have access to information on her life that no one else will. This information is precious and needs to be incorporated into the assessment and care plan.

- *Ignoring* for example, talking only to Mrs Hardy's daughter, acting as if Mrs Hardy were not present or was too incapacitated to meaningfully contribute to the conversation.

- *Disruption* for example, breaking into Mrs Hardy's conversation or train of thought. It may be that you have a number of visits to conduct or have to be at your next appointment soon. That is your problem and you need to consider how you manage your time better. What Mrs Hardy needs at this point in her life is time to reflect, ask questions and communicate in her own way at her own pace.

- *Mockery* making fun of inappropriate or tangential comments made by Mrs Hardy, perhaps encouraging flippant or demeaning comments from her daughter.

- *Disparagement* not respecting information provided by Mrs Hardy, giving her negative messages about her self or her future which undermine her confidence and self-esteem.

(adapted from Kitwood 1997, pp46–7)

So far in our case study we have concentrated on the importance of communication and how good communication skills can help to develop relationships and promote *personhood.*

I want us to look at a different aspect of spirituality in older age now by considering some of the issues regarding *transcending loss*.

The experience of change and loss

Mrs Hardy remains at home and is well supported by the care package that you have arranged. Unfortunately, she has a fall and fractures her hip. After a period of hospitalisation, her confusion increases and the decision is taken that she can no longer manage at home and needs to go into residential care.

The potential losses faced by Mrs Hardy as she leaves her home and moves into residential care could be considerable. Some will be obvious and profound while others will be less noticeable. All, however, have the potential to adversely impact on her spiritual well-being. Equally, we need to be balanced and recognise that not all losses she will experience will be negative and that there are some gains to entering residential care.

ACTIVITY 4.2

Make a list of the potential losses that Mrs Hardy may face when she leaves her home and enters residential care. Identify the spiritual aspects of these losses.

Here are two examples to help you make a start.

- *Mrs Hardy will lose contact with people from her community. The next-door neighbours, her GP, the milkman, the boy who delivers her newspaper, the young mother and her children who pass her house every day on the way to school and wave to her. The spiritual impact will be that Mrs Hardy will lose relationships that may appear to be tenuous but nonetheless are important to her. She will also lose a sense of belonging to her community.*

- *Mrs Hardy will lose many of her possessions as they will not fit into her small bedroom at the home. The spiritual impact will be that she will lose part of her history and identity, for example the wardrobe that belonged to her mother and the painting given to her by her husband.*

Let me give you two more examples of the type of change and loss that Mrs Hardy may experience.

Space can be important to us, particularly space which we own and have adapted for our own pleasure or purpose. It may be that the garden at the bungalow is of considerable significance to Mrs Hardy. It is overgrown now but once was the pride and joy of her husband who planted many of the shrubs and trees that continue to flourish within it. Once the property is sold, the garden will be lost to her and may be altered significantly by new owners. Her husband's ashes are scattered under the willow tree that he planted at the bottom of the garden. Until recently, Mrs Hardy liked to spend time sitting under the tree remembering her husband.

The spiritual losses to Mrs Hardy are obvious. She will lose an important connection to her husband, part of her identity as a person and a visual reminder of happier times in her life. As a social worker it is unlikely that you will be in a position to transplant a garden or move a tree, but there may be some practical things that you can do to assist Mrs Hardy.

As Mrs Hardy's social worker you should have identified the significance of the garden, and the willow tree, as part of your holistic assessment. And it would be important to pass on that information to the staff at the residential home. The home may well have a garden or a park nearby where Mrs Hardy could revisit her memories. Good spiritual care is often based on the ordinary everyday experiences that we can take for granted. The feel of the wind, the colour of the sky, the beauty of flowers and casual conversation with strangers. Sometimes older people, due to their frailty and perhaps a lack of staff in care settings, get little opportunity to enjoy these simple pleasures. If this aspect of life is important to Mrs Hardy it is essential that those who you are commissioning to care for her are fully aware of that fact.

One carer who supported her husband for many years through the experience of Alzheimer's similarly noted that he:

> . . . *seemed to gain a deep pleasure from nature – colours of flowers, textures of leaves, movement of water, shapes in the sunsets – and from simple things like tastes of food, collecting stones, walks, holding hands, smiley faces. With cognition failing, and function dwindling, a new importance was being attached to the sensory and emotional.*

> (Pointon, 2007, p116)

In Chapter 3 we spoke about the importance of art and how involvement in art projects such as STEER and 'Call that singing?' could positively affect both individual participants and communities. Creativity is a gift that sustains and nourishes the human spirit and its absence is to be regretted. It may be that Mrs Hardy is a gifted musician who spent many hours playing her piano in her bungalow. The piano is large and heavy and will not fit into the residential home. Equally, she feels self-conscious playing in front of other people and it is likely that she will not play again once she leaves her bungalow. As a busy professional you may feel that this is not your problem. Let me encourage you to think again.

The move from her home into residential care is a crisis for Mrs Hardy. The transition will be considerable involving change and disruption, and she will need all her resources to successfully manage the move. One of those resources is her musicality which has helped to define who she is and has been a source of comfort to her over the years. As her social worker one of your roles will be to prepare the staff at the home and work with them to facilitate the transition. Part of that work would be to identify that Mrs Hardy enjoys playing the piano and liaising with the home as to how they can encourage her to keep playing. The home may already have a piano in a room which is not often used or may have access to a church hall with a piano which Mrs Hardy could visit.

Holistic assessment

On a number of occasions in this chapter I have alluded to the phrase holistic assessment. In recent years this has become something of a buzzword in social work and refers to assessment processes which take into account the whole person, that is the physical, emotional and environmental needs of the service user. Service user and carer participation is explicit in such an assessment and the focus is on participation and empowerment. The views and expertise of other professionals are elicited and incorporated into the assessment. All of these facets come together in the assessment which gives a view of the whole person in their social context. Social work has traditionally viewed itself as being a profession that has embraced holistic practice. Holistic emphases, however, are not unique to social work and are equally important in other professions such as nursing and palliative care.

The culture of holistic assessment is to be welcomed and encouraged as it moves away from the deficit model that has characterised adult care assessments in the past. Too often we have focused on what service users cannot do and have failed to recognise their many strengths and resources. To an extent the system of community care with its emphasis on prioritising resources to those most in need has led social workers to overemphasise the vulnerability of service users in order to access resources. The above exercise concerning Mrs Hardy neatly demonstrates the point, for we have spent a considerable amount of time talking about what she will lose and implicitly what she cannot do for herself anymore. We have not spent too much time considering those abilities and gifts which make her uniquely who she is. One of the responsibilities of being a social worker is that you must strive to produce a balanced assessment which includes both the strengths and weaknesses of a service user.

What has often been omitted from assessments in past times, however, is an assessment of spiritual need. Recently, the situation has improved with assessment documentation giving at least some space to spiritual need, but sometimes this has been perfunctory and poorly completed by assessors who are ill-equipped or too embarrassed to talk about spirituality. In nursing, particularly in North America, there is a growing requirement that nurses take a spiritual history alongside a physical health history when patients are admitted to hospital.

Similarly, I would encourage you as a social worker undertaking a holistic assessment to think about the spiritual needs and resources that all service users have and need to access, especially at times of crisis. You may find it helpful to consider the following questions.

- What gifts, insights and resources does the service user use to sustain and nourish their spirit? Like Mrs Hardy, this may be music or art. It could be attendance at a place of worship, or a myriad of simple things that provide life with meaning.

- How can these be identified? What do you need to do to identify these resources?

- Who will help you identify these resources? An obvious place to start is with the person themselves, but relatives and friends may also provide invaluable information.

Black elders

I have deliberately not said anything about Mrs Hardy's race or ethnicity. You may have made the assumption that she is a white woman. But what would be the implications if she were Black?

It could well be that her experience of life has been very different to that of an older white person and could have been characterised by migration, separation from family, racism and exclusion.

Faith, stories and the experience of Black elders

Anthony Reddie is a Black theologian and academic who has written extensively on the experiences of older African-Caribbean people in Britain.

He raises a number of issues which are important for us to consider as social workers interested in spirituality.

- Firstly, the importance of the oral tradition and storytelling in Caribbean culture. As we will see later, storytelling can be an effective way of recalling memories, expressing truths about our lives and informing the younger generation about the struggles, joys and trials of earlier times. Sometimes in Western culture the oral tradition is neglected or seen as inferior to the written word. In African culture, however, the oral tradition is the main vehicle through which the essential nature of Black existence and experience has been channelled. On many occasions, the history and contribution of Black people has been ignored and neglected by official historians. Story telling remains a potent way that the lives of marginalised people can be *affirmed, celebrated and confirmed.*

- Reddie also reminds us that many Caribbean people believe in a God who is present with them in their daily lives, a companion who hears and listens to their prayers and is a witness to their trials and struggles. The Christian church has been a symbol of liberation for them, one of the few places where they could freely express themselves during the days of slavery. This is tangibly different to the distant God worshipped by many white Christians where an emphasis is placed, as the hymn writer puts it, on the God who resides in 'light inaccessible hid from our eyes'.

- Migration is an ever-present theme in the physical and spiritual lives of many older African-Caribbean people. The majority of older Black people in Britain were born outside the UK and came to this country to provide a better life for themselves and their children. Often families were divided by migration, and

→

> **Faith, stories and the experience of Black elders,** *continued*
>> sometimes people do not feel at home either in Britain or the Caribbean. It is telling that the sub-title to one of Reddie's books is 'Singing the Lord's song in a strange land' which echoes the feelings of estrangement felt by the people of Israel when they were removed from their homeland in the Old Testament.
>
> - The legacy of slavery survives in the way that Black people have internalised the message that they are inferior and of little importance. The daily experience of racism confirms and strengthens this legacy. Any oppressive experience is corrosive to the physical, emotional and spiritual well-being of the individual and denies personhood.
>
>> (adapted from Reddie, 2001)

I hope that you can see from these very brief notes that many of the issues we have raised in this chapter would need to be revisited and reinterpreted if Mrs Hardy was a Black elder. For example, her identity as a Black woman living in a predominantly white society could be difficult to decipher. There may be few people who could meaningfully *celebrate, affirm and confirm* her journey through life due to a lack of knowledge or understanding. It may be that Mrs Hardy is part of the *Windrush* generation – those first immigrants from the Caribbean who came to Britain in the late 1940s. This fact alone would set her apart and be integral to who she is, why she is where she is and how she interprets her life.

Seeking final meaning

Throughout this chapter we have talked about the *spiritual tasks of ageing.* One of these tasks assumes greater significance in older age – that of making sense of life, finding out who we really are or seeking final meaning to one's existence. Encountering loss and change is an integral part of human experience and is by no means exclusive to older people. What we can say is that older age is often a time when change and loss accelerates and people may need to review or evaluate their life. A number of theorists of human development, for example Erikson, highlight this stage of life as being one where the person grapples with the question, has my life been worthwhile?

RESEARCH SUMMARY

Erik Erikson on late adulthood

Erik Erikson (1902–94) was a psychologist and psychoanalyst who had a life-long interest in human identity. He developed a theory of human development based on eight sequential stages through which people had to pass if they were to lead fulfilled lives.

Erikson's final stage of life is entitled 'late adulthood' where the person seeks to achieve a sense of wholeness and an acceptance of past decisions and life events. If the person can gain a measure of peace and acceptance, a feeling that their life has been worthwhile, this enables them to face death without regret or disillusionment.

(Crawford and Walker, 2003, p111)

As a social worker in adult care it is likely you will find that people will share profound questions about their lives with you. You may not be able to provide a ready response to these questions as human experience is rarely straightforward. This reviewing of life is a spiritual activity as it helps to confirm who we are as people and provides an opportunity for *affirmation, celebration and confirmation.* There are many ways in which people may invite you to share in the story of their lives, and there are a number of tools you can use to enable people to review their lives.

In recent years there has been increased interest in reminiscence work and life review with older people. I have provided the context why this work is of importance and why some older people will benefit from an approach that assists them to review and evaluate their life. It is not within the scope of this book to offer more than a few ideas as to the general skills that you may utilise as a social worker in this type of role.

RESEARCH SUMMARY

Telling stories
Working with groups is a skill that you should develop as a social worker. Group work used to be a popular therapeutic tool in the 1960s and 1970s but declined in popularity as one-to-one casework took precedence. I am pleased to say that it appears to have had a revival in usage over the last few years and is incorporated into the National Occupational Standards and is increasingly being taught on university social work courses. For some service users, participating in a group can be a very affirming way of sharing experiences and developing awareness of their situation. As always, the greater the number of tools you have at your disposal as a social worker, the more effective you are likely to be.

Group work with older people with dementia has often been a valuable way of gently encouraging people to share some of their stories. Some researchers suggest that people do not randomly recall past events but that their chosen stories are rich in metaphor and shed light on their current situation.

For example, one man with dementia recalled his wartime experiences in Malaya. His abiding memory was of continually having to hack back the jungle vegetation which seemed to make any sort of journey difficult. This was seen as a way for him to relate to his struggle with dementia and the way in which it has made life's journey increasingly difficult for him.

(Adapted from Kitwood, 1997, p74)

Comment

Inviting people to review their past through telling their own story is one possible tool that you may wish to use. Great sensitivity and skill is required to do this and it should not be entered into lightly.

Other creative methods you could consider include:

- **The use of objects such as photographs, ornaments, or letters to stimulate memory or discussion.**

- **The use of drawing**   Some reminiscence work invites people to draw episodes or events from their lives. The artwork produced need not be polished or professional but can be a powerful way of celebrating and affirming life events. For example, one older woman I worked with drew a picture of the day her father returned from the Second World War. The drawing captured the spirit of the day with flags, bunting, people rushing about, crowds pushing and shoving. In the corner was one little lost girl desperately searching the throng for her daddy. While it may be speculative, I believe that the picture offered a review of a past significant event, and also gave me an insight into that service user's current state of mind: her desire for comfort, reassurance and the presence of a familiar figure.

- **The use of music**   Music in particular is very emotive and can reach people when words are no longer accessible to them. Sometimes it is better to sit in silence with a person and listen to a piece of music that is of particular significance to them than to attempt to engage them in conversation.

These are only a few of the ways in which you may seek to engage with a person who wants to explore the purpose of their life. There are many more and it would be unwise to be prescriptive as to how you may do it. I am not suggesting that as a social worker you need to become an expert in art or reminiscence therapy – although people sometimes underestimate the range of skills required to be an effective social worker. But you do need to consider how you might help someone who is seeking to find *final meaning*.

C H A P T E R   S U M M A R Y

Part of my intention in this chapter was to provide a framework to help you to meet the social work Subject Benchmark 5.1.1 which requires you to understand:

> the social processes (in this case the social processes associated with ageing and in particular older people) that lead to marginalisation, isolation and exclusion, and their impact on the demand for social work services.

You have achieved this through reading the chapter and completing the exercises which have offered a rounded view of the connections between spirituality and social work with older people. For example, you started the chapter by looking at some of the spiritual tasks associated with ageing. Many of these tasks identify psychological 'work to be done' but also offer a way of celebrating and affirming life.

You then looked at dementia and how the social processes that can sometimes characterise the care provided to people with cognitive impairment can lead to marginalisation, isolation and exclusion. As writers such as Shamy and Kitwood remind us, sometimes people who have dementia are viewed as being of less value. In particular, the work of Kitwood on malignant social psychology emphasised some of the ways in which older people can have their well-being undermined by care which disables and oppresses.

An extended case study on Mrs Hardy was then used to tease out some of the practicalities and skills that you require to be an efficient and thoughtful worker in adult care. Throughout this chapter we have referred back to the tasks of ageing identified by MacKinlay and Jewell as a way of framing our discussion. Social work practice with adults is extremely pressurised and is often characterised by outcomes, targets and a lack of resources. I hope that this chapter has served to balance your thinking and introduce you to a better way of practice.

Baldwin, C and Capstick, A (eds) (2007) *Tom Kitwood on dementia: A reader and critical commentary.* Buckingham: Open University Press.
I hope that this chapter and the references I have made to the important work undertaken by Professor Tom Kitwood has whetted your appetite to explore his work in greater detail. This edited text provides a balanced view of his contribution.

Crawford, K and Walker, J (2008) *Social work with older people,* 2nd edition. Exeter: Learning Matters.
This is an excellent and accessible introduction to working with older people. Chapter 1 on values and ethics is particularly appropriate as it talks about many issues that touch on spirituality, such as dignity and empowerment.

Cunningham, J and Cunningham, S (2008) *Sociology and social work.* Exeter: Learning Matters.
As a sociologist I recognise that I am biased, but there are clear links between the discipline and the practice of social work that need to be reiterated and maintained. This book provides a thoughtful introduction which will help you make connections to the context of contemporary practice.

MacKinlay, E (2008) *Ageing, disability and spirituality: Addressing the challenge of disability in later life.* London: Jessica Kingsley.
This is a collection of essays that provides an accessible introduction to later life and spirituality.

Dementia positive www.dementiapositive.co.uk
This is the website of John Killick and Kate Allan who have worked creatively with people with cognitive impairment for many years. The site contains information about their work and their many publications. In particular, the authors have established a reputation for encouraging people with Alzheimer's to write poetry expressing their feelings and celebrating their lives.

Chapter 5

Working with spirituality: Disability

This chapter will help you meet the following National Occupational Standards:

Key Role 1: Prepare for, and work with individuals, families, carers, groups and communities to assess their needs and circumstances.

- Work with individuals, families, carers, groups and communities to identify, gather, analyse and understand information.
- Work with individuals, families, carers, groups and communities to enable them to analyse, identify, clarify and express their strengths, expectations and limitations.
- Work with individuals, families, carers, groups and communities to enable them to assess and make informed decisions about their needs, circumstances, risks, preferred options and resources.

It will also introduce you to the following academic standards as set out in the Subject Benchmark Statement for social work.

5.1.1 Social work services, service users and carers.
- The social processes (associated with, for example, poverty, migration, unemployment, poor health, disablement, lack of education and other sources of disadvantage) that lead to marginalisation, isolation and exclusion, and their impact on the demand for social work services.
- Explanations of the links between definitional processes contributing to social differences (for example, social class, gender, ethnic differences, age, sexuality and religious belief) to the problems of inequality and differential need faced by service users.
- The nature of social work services in a diverse society (with particular reference to concepts such as prejudice, interpersonal, institutional and structural discrimination, empowerment and anti-discriminatory practices).

5.1.3 Values and ethics.
- The nature, historical evolution and application of social work values.

5.1.5 The nature of social work practice.
- The nature and characteristics of skills associated with effective practice, both direct and indirect, with a range of service users and in a variety of settings.
- The processes that facilitate and support service user choice and independence.

Introduction

Throughout this book I have argued that all people have spiritual needs and that spirituality is a significant dimension of humanity which needs to be addressed within social work practice. This is particularly relevant in social work with disabled people whose collective and individual spiritual needs have often been overlooked or discounted. In this chapter, I will briefly explore this disregard and suggest ways in which social work with disabled people might incorporate a more spiritually aware approach.

You may remember from my introduction to the previous chapter that there has been relatively little work undertaken on spirituality and disability. In my view, this reflects the low priority and status sometimes given to working with people with disability by health and social care organisations where the needs of higher-profile groups, such as children, are seen to be of more importance. Interest in spirituality and disability, however, continues to increase and it is to be hoped that more work will be published over the coming years. Nonetheless, it is valuable to explore the context and nuances within which social work practice with disabled people occurs. Good social work practice depends on a balanced understanding of context and the structural pressures that define the lives of service users.

We will also be implicitly alluding to holistic ways of working throughout this chapter. This is where the needs of body, mind and spirit are recognised and are seen as having equal worth. While the growth of holistic work is by no means confined to social work or to work with disabled people, it is of some significance and represents good professional practice.

I also want to encourage you to spend some time thinking about your own spiritual awareness and practice, and how this might be affected by the organisation you work for. Social workers rarely operate as solitary practitioners but instead operate within the context of being employed by organisations which facilitate either good or poor spiritual care by the way in which they treat and equip their employees. This organic view mirrors some of the thinking we have undertaken in previous chapters. For example, we have emphasised the importance of community in creating a spiritual climate. If a person lives in a spiritually corrosive community with little solidarity or sense of belonging, it is unlikely that they will feel spiritually vibrant. In the same way, if as a social worker you are employed by an organisation which is little more than a soulless bureaucratic machine, it is unlikely that spiritually aware practice will be acknowledged or encouraged. To borrow a phrase from the seventeenth-century poet, John Donne, *No man is an island* (Alford, 1839, p574). We do not work in isolation and our professional practice will be informed by the nature of the organisation that we work for.

But firstly, as the only way we can interpret the present is by exploring the past, I want to discuss the historical lack of interest that there has been in meeting the spiritual needs of people with disabilities.

Ambivalence and disregard

Historically people with learning disabilities have been viewed in a number of competing ways. For example, it has been suggested that in the Middle Ages:

> *People with an intellectual disability were either viewed as possessed by the devil and persecuted, or cared for and sheltered in monasteries. Still others found their place as court jesters, pets, or as companions for noblemen, for they were believed to possess special skills as oracles.*

(Selway and Ashman, 1998, p431)

In ancient Greece the Spartans killed disabled children by throwing them from the cliffs, while in North America the Saulteaux tribe would murder disabled infants believing them to be possessed by evil spirits. In other cultures, however, disabled people were treated with greater respect and sometimes viewed as having insights and powers not available to the able bodied (Selway and Ashman, 1998, p431).

It is also worth remembering that historically in the West, and especially in the United Kingdom, the care of disabled people has been characterised by institutionalisation, segregation and exclusion from mainstream society. From the advent of early Poor Law legislation in the sixteenth century until the latter decades of the twentieth century, people with physical or learning disabilities and mental health problems were often incarcerated in large-scale hospitals which were situated some distance outside major towns. Many people lived in these institutions for years, sometimes decades, with little prospect of contact or integration with able-bodied society. Life would often be dominated by routine, rules and structures which were dehuman-ising and inflexible. The larger hospitals would have their own amenities including tennis courts, gardens, laundry facilities, shops and chapel. It is difficult to imagine what effect these institutionalised living arrangements would have on people. I suggest that it would be difficult to retain a sense of identity and lead a life characterised by purpose, fulfilment and meaning. Consequently, institutions could be spiritually damaging places to live, although some did place an emphasis on rehabilitation and equipping people to live back in the community. Social workers were instrumental in maintaining these oppressive care arrangements and it is interesting to see how both the views of society concerning institutional care and the role of social work have changed over time.

In the twenty-first century we like to think that we have moved beyond these historical views and ways of working. The emphasis in contemporary adult care is to support disabled people to remain at home through the provision of care packages and more innovative ways of meeting identified need, such as Direct Payments. Personalisation and choice are now buzzwords in adult care and, it could be argued, disabled people have a greater level of resource allocation and choice than at any time. The old institutions have gone and disabled people have a greater presence in the community than at any time in the recent past.

Nonetheless, I would argue that in contemporary society people with disabilities continue to lead lives characterised by exclusion and marginalisation. Disabled people may no longer live 'out of sight and out of mind', but the end of large-scale institutional care has not always led to increased opportunities. Institutionalised care arrangements do not need an institution to survive. A disabled person's bedsit in an anonymous tower block can be as limiting as any Victorian institution. Disabled people continue to be excluded from mainstream education, leisure facilities and employment opportunities that able-bodied people often take for granted. As we reflected in Chapter 3, communities can be hostile and uncomfortable places for some people to live. While there have been significant changes in public attitudes towards disabled people in recent decades, some disabled people still feel disregarded and threatened within their own communities.

Bergant (1994) goes further still and argues that people with disabilities do not, indeed cannot, conform to the perceived idea of what it is to be 'normal'. Consequently, they are actively marginalised, even punished for their lack of conformity by able-bodied society.

Too often they are regarded as less than human, their movement is restricted, their existence is circumscribed, and they are denied access to much that society offers for a fulfilling life.

(Bergant, 1994, p21)

This may appear to be an extreme position but it is reflected by other commentators. For example, Jean Vanier, the founder of the L'Arche community, refers to learning disabled people giving a primal cry of pain at their oppression and mistreatment. Vanier argues from a Christian position that all people have an element of God within them and that it is a duty to seek that worth and goodness (Vanier, 1995). While some may not be happy with the overt religious terminology employed by Vanier, his promotion of equality and respect is to be valued. You may also reflect that there are clear connections with the work of Tom Kitwood that we used in the previous chapter.

ACTIVITY 5.1

Consider the comments of Bergant and Vanier. If (learning) disabled people are oppressed and ignored by society, how can their spirituality and spiritual lives be enhanced?

Comment

You will recall that one of the National Occupational Standards (2.3) highlighted at the commencement of the chapter suggests that social work needs to enable people to *express their strengths, expectations and limitations*. What I would like you to consider is that enabling marginalised people to express themselves, to articulate their strengths and *to find a voice* is both a core function of social work and a spiritual task. This is sometimes not easy as marginalised people rarely have the opportunities or the resources to articulate their needs. Active participation and partnership that goes beyond tokenism are all prerequisites of good social work practice. In themselves they are purely a start, but if they enable disabled people to exercise more control and choice over their lives it will go some way to promoting their spirituality.

RESEARCH SUMMARY

Negative images of learning disability

The writers I have referred to above argue that how we see people and the contribution they make to life often determines how much they are valued and respected. If we feel that someone is important, or that their contribution to society is of high value, we tend to treat them with respect and dignity. For example, in terms of occupation, people like doctors and lawyers are often seen as being more important than people who work in unskilled jobs.

Conversely, if the prevailing view is that some people, or groups of people, do not contribute much or are of no importance, they are treated with less respect. I appreciate that this is a simplistic understanding of a complex subject, but as a general rule disabled people are often devalued in our culture where health, beauty, youth and being able-bodied is explicitly valued. Again, you should be able to make a connection to previous comments we made regarding the devaluing of older people.

The influential American psychologist Wolf Wolfensberger suggests that this devaluation and lack of regard stems from the stereotypical way in which people with learning disabilities are viewed by society. These are:

- *as a sick person needing care and attention from others;*
- *as a subhuman organism not fit to thrive or perform as a full human being;*
- *as a menace to society needing to be monitored and controlled;*
- *as an object of pity;*
- *as a burden needing charity and indulgence from others;*
- *as a holy innocent who lacks understanding or malice.*

(Williams, 2006)

Religion and disability

Throughout history, the main religions have provided care and support to people with disabilities, but have also been guilty of oppressing and marginalising them. For example, Smalley (2001) traces the evolution of Christian care for disabled people in the United States and argues that the large institutions provided by the church were designed to keep disabled people beyond public view. It was not until after the two world wars in the twentieth century, when large numbers of disabled service personnel returned from the front, that people with disability became more visible in society.

In contemporary Christianity some people with learning disability are refused Holy Communion (that is the ritual taking of bread and wine which symbolically re-enacts the Last Supper of Jesus and his disciples) on the basis that they do not understand the full significance of what they are doing. For similar reasons, others are refused or never offered full church membership.

CASE STUDY

Elizabeth Mosely is a disabled activist who comes from a Christian background in Australia. Her powerful story relates how as a newly disabled person she felt marginalised and excluded from many aspects of worship which she had previously taken for granted. She views her spiritual journey as being one of solitary confinement, where consistently she has been unable to engage in collective church activities due to her disability. As a wheelchair user she is often unable to fully access places of worship and finds herself trapped behind pillars and pews if she is able to get into a building. As an activist she campaigns not only for herself, but also for other disabled people. She gives a number of examples of oppression and exclusion and offers this challenge:

I have not lost my spirituality, simply my ability to walk. The very process of ageing causes an ever increasing number of problems with access for a regrettably large number of people. And these people have often given a lifetime of service to their church and to their faith. One day they are there in their usual pew, and the next, they have had to accept the unpalatable reality that they no longer have the right to worship with others. That perpetual struggle to manage even a few steps has beaten them. Their faith has not diminished either, only their mobility.

(Mosely, 2004, pp118–19)

ACTIVITY 5.2

This example from Elizabeth Mosely is clearly set within a faith context but echoes a wider point that disabled people often feel ignored and excluded from mainstream life due to a lack of access. This is not purely physical access but may also be a reflection of the fact that disabled people are sometimes not welcomed or accepted by non-disabled people.

I would like you to spend some time now reflecting on non-religious aspects of spirituality. Make a list of situations or places of spiritual significance that could be difficult to access for someone with a disability.

Comment

I am sure that on reflection you had no difficulty making a list as there are so many places and situations that could be inaccessible or where disabled people are made to feel uncomfortable or unwelcome.

For example:

- ***Places where people gather together for shared activities such as theatres, leisure centres or cinemas*** communal activity is an important means of creating relationship and confirming identity. Often older buildings are difficult to physically access and sometimes disabled people can be inappropriately placed, either segregated in a corner of the building or conspicuously seated at the front. Sometimes there is also an air of disregard or even hostility directed towards disabled people at public gatherings. For example, I have heard obscene chants directed at people in wheelchairs at football grounds and have had to endure thoughtless and hostile remarks when taking learning disabled people to the cinema.

- *The countryside*   enjoying the solitude and beauty of the countryside can be a very healing experience and reminds us of our place in the world. While considerable efforts have been made in recent years to make more footpaths and routes more wheelchair-friendly it is difficult for disabled people to participate equally in the countryside with non-disabled friends.

- *Accessing other people's homes*   even a simple pleasure like attending a family gathering can be difficult, especially if the bathroom is upstairs!

I appreciate that many public buildings are now fully accessible and that public attitudes towards the inclusion of disabled people may be changing, but the point remains: Often disabled people have to struggle to access opportunities which strengthen and enrich their spiritual lives.

The professional disregard of spiritual needs

Given this history it should not be a surprise to learn that professionals working in health and social care settings have also been guilty of disregarding the spiritual needs of disabled people.

I will be referring to the work of Narayanasamy, et al. (2002) on a number of occasions in this chapter. Their area of research is with learning disability nurses. While we always need to be cautious about extrapolating from other disciplines, I suggest that what they have to say is of relevance to social work. For example, they found that learning disability nurses did not give adequate attention to the provision of spiritual care, and that there was confusion in their minds as to what spirituality was and how it fitted with their professional role. Other non-nursing colleagues on the ward, such as care and support workers, were similarly inadequately equipped to recognise and work with spirituality. The authors provide a number of reasons why this might be the case, one of which is particularly relevant to social work.

They suggest that a lack of awareness of your own spirituality can be a stumbling block to the recognition and provision of good spiritual care. This is an important point which I want us to explore in some detail. In order to help us, I have devised a case study which I would like you to read before completing the reflective exercise that follows.

CASE STUDY

Zahra is a 40-year-old woman who is originally from Iran. She has been admitted to a residential home for emergency respite care following a deterioration in her health. She acquired a significant physical disability following a broken spine in a road traffic accident ten years ago. She is a wheelchair user and only has limited movement in one arm and hand. Zahra is described as being low in spirit and lives alone in an adapted bungalow on a large housing estate. She is single and rarely sees her family following a major disagreement some years ago. Ordinarily she manages well with support from a personal assistant employed via Direct Payments.

The case has been allocated to you as a social worker and you have been asked by your team manager to undertake an assessment of her needs. You are extremely busy at work and arrive an hour late for your first appointment with her. You apologise profusely but are aware that you have another appointment at the opposite end of the town in less than an hour. In order to save time you decide to interview Zahra in the lounge. There are a couple of other people present but they appear to be asleep. You produce the assessment documentation and proceed to undertake a functional assessment. Due to the lack of time you are writing furiously, anxious not to miss any vital information. Zahra, however, has not seen anyone all day and is keen to talk about herself and her background. In particular, she has a long held interest in Zoroastrianism and wonders if her car accident was caused because of something which she had done in her early life. She also seems to want to explore her complicated family background as she had seen someone in the town the previous week who looked like her brother who she used to be very close to. She has not had any contact with him for several years, but would like you to help her think about the wisdom of trying to get back in touch with him. You, however, have no time for such distractions and are anxious to complete the paperwork in order to meet the deadline for the resource allocation panel which will allocate funding for Zahra's stay.

The spiritually-aware social worker

I hope that your practice is nothing like the picture I have portrayed as service users deserve a far better service from professionals employed to work in partnership with them. In recent years, the government has introduced a number of developments designed to raise standards within social work. For example, social workers are now required to register with their professional body, the General Social Care Council, and to abide by a code of professional conduct. The title of social worker is protected by law and the professional qualification is now a three-year degree programme. All of these developments have undoubtedly raised the profile of social work, but has it led to a better standard of practice? The answer to that question lies outside of the remit of this book, but it would be interesting to consider if this increased professionalism has encouraged, or impeded, spiritual awareness and good spiritual practice among the profession.

ACTIVITY **5.3**

I want you to consider the case study you have just read and answer three related questions connected to the provision of social work practice which recognises the importance of spirituality.

Consider these questions and make some notes:

• Did Zahra receive good spiritual care from her social worker?

• How would a service user know that they had received good spiritual care from a social worker?

• What awareness, skills and knowledge does a social worker need in order to provide good spiritual care?

Comment

Zahra seems to be at a vulnerable time in her life where she requires a thoughtful and humane response from her social worker. Yet all she gets is someone who is late, has no time to offer and is obsessed with procedures and form filling. So, do you think that Zahra received good spiritual care from her social worker? I do not think that she did. In order to tease out the reasons for this we also need to consider the second question: How would a service user know that they had received good spiritual care? This is what some colleagues said when I asked them.

A service user would know that they had received good spiritual care if the social worker had:

• not hidden behind professional expertise or processes but had taken time to really listen to the person's worries and concerns;

• been open and honest about their limitations; acknowledging that social workers have feelings too and can be vulnerable;

• talked to the service user about their life in the past, present and future;

• valued the information given and respected the decisions made by the person;

• communicated in a variety of ways, including eye contact, smiling, possibly touch;

• reacted as a fellow human being to expressed emotions such as distress and uncertainty;

• committed themselves to the service user for the duration of their involvement through the development of a relationship which had meaning for both people;

• given acknowledgement, affirmation and unconditional positive regard.

I felt that these responses were interesting and that they proved that Zahra's social worker had not provided good spiritual care. He or she may well have completed the assessment documentation thoroughly and efficiently but they barely engaged with Zahra as a fellow human being. The responses simply emphasise how crucial human relationships are to good social work practice. The ability to connect with another human being, to engage with their emotions and to empathise with their vulnerability is one of the greatest skills of the caring professions.

Some of the points raised, however, do require further discussion. For example, the use of touch as a form of communication is problematical in social work as it can be open to interpretation, is not universally welcomed and may even be exploitative. Zahra may not welcome being touched, especially if her social worker is male. This is not to say that touch should never be used, as holding someone's hand or lightly touching them on the arm can be an effective way of connecting with someone in distress. What it does mean is that it should only be used wisely and discretely.

I tried to answer the third question and felt that it was difficult to separate awareness, skills and knowledge as all three seemed to be interconnected. In terms of skills I expect that some of you thought about:

- relationship building;
- empathy;
- the use of a range of communication skills;
- creativity;
- time management;
- cultural sensitivity.

All of these skills are of course underpinned by knowledge. For example, why is it important to use a range of communication skills? Because we know that some people find the spoken word difficult to understand. They may have a disability which impacts on their understanding, or a hearing impairment, or have difficulty understanding English/Welsh. It may be, for example, that Zahra has learnt English relatively recently and may struggle with the complexities of professional jargon. We also know that non-verbal communication, such as body posture, facial expression and mannerisms, reveal a lot about the way people are feeling and as social workers we need to be aware of what messages we are conveying and receiving.

What I want you to see is that self-awareness and an awareness of your own spirituality is essential to the delivery of good spiritual care. Skills and knowledge in themselves will not be enough if awareness is absent. This perhaps is again best understood by posing a question. How can you provide good spiritual care if you have no awareness of your own spirituality? That is, an understanding of what makes you tick, your beliefs and values, your motivation in life, what makes you uniquely who you are and your identity as a person? Integral to this is an understanding of why the world is like it is. As we have already discussed, religion may inform our view of the world, as may other ideologies such as socialism or feminism. Other worldviews may be less coherent or well formed, but nonetheless all are valid.

I am sure that some of you will have experienced a sense of *déjà vu* reading the last couple of paragraphs as there are commonalities with the points made using the scenario of Mrs Hardy in the previous chapter. Underpinning practice skills is the same across social work as the ability to communicate, self-awareness and good professional judgement are all key components of successful social work intervention. There may well be some repetition within the book as my argument remains consistent throughout: that social work needs to incorporate spiritual awareness if it is to be effective in facilitating lasting change.

I appreciate that this view is a challenge for those who struggle to understand the implications of spirituality or for people who are still finding their way in the world. Spiritual awareness is not something that can develop overnight and life experience is vital in helping to fashion our understanding of ourselves and of the world. All of us are on a journey of self-development where experience, maturity, training and the influence of other people will help to develop our understanding. Some are further along that journey than others, and I would not want you to feel disheartened if other people appear to have developed a greater sense of self-awarenesst than you. What I would encourage you to consider, however, is that education is not merely about the acquisition of skills and knowledge, but is also about transformation and personal growth.

Professional development and reflective practice

One of the key skills of social work is reflective practice, that is taking time to critically review an action or intervention and learn lessons from it – like we have just done with the fictional case of Zahra.

It is important to reflect on both good and poor practice, so that next time you undertake a similar task you will be better prepared and able to adopt a more skilful approach. Sometimes it is useful to do this reflection with another colleague or your practice learning assessor as their insights may well be different to yours.

This questioning approach should be adopted both before and after an event, and is only useful if the lessons learnt are put into practice. For example, if the social worker had thought about the visit to Zahra beforehand they might have avoided some of the poor practice that was displayed. In particular, they should have considered issues of race, language and gender and thoughtfully considered how they could appropriately engage with Zahra – particularly in a communal living environment.

Equally, taking time to review a visit that has not gone well can provide a significant amount of learning. Reflection is also a spiritual activity. Examining ourselves, our value base and our actions touches on our core understanding of life and who we are, and inevitably changes us both personally and professionally. Reflection is a skill which sometimes does not come easily to busy social workers but is a cornerstone of professional development.

(Adapted from Horner, 2003, pp9–10)

The benefits of spiritually-aware practice

Throughout this book I have argued that practice which enhances spirituality is beneficial to both communities and individual service users. Service users and patients indicate that they appreciate good spiritual care when they receive it. For example, in a research study previously referred to by Narayanasamy, et al. (2002) both learning disabled people and their families felt that care received from nurses who provided time, space, conversation, and a peaceful unhurried environment was both strengthening and comforting.

> *Following spiritual care interventions, clients appeared peaceful, relaxed, and calm . . . Such states would aid clients' healing and recovery, or peaceful death.*
>
> (p955)

All of these ways of working recognise the importance of holistic intervention and promote a sense of well-being. You may reflect how simple these approaches were but how difficult to put into practice on hectic wards or in busy organisations driven by targets and outcomes.

But it is not only service users or patients who gain from the provision of spiritual care. Practitioners also receive rewards and benefits.

ACTIVITY **5.5**

I want you to think about a situation you have been involved in where you have provided care to someone else. It may have been formally at school or at work, or maybe informally to a friend or relative. What motivated you to care for that person?

Comment

I imagine that some of you found that exercise to be quite straightforward while others may have struggled. Sometimes it is difficult to tease out the reasons why we do something. It may be that some of you felt obliged to care through ties of friendship and relationship. Some of you may have been paid to provide care or rewarded in other ways. Still others may have felt coerced or that there was simply no one else around to do the job.

What motivates and rewards practitioners in the caring professions is also difficult to explore. Often caring work is modestly paid and of low status compared with other professions. While few people explicitly enter social work to receive thanks and praise, knowing that you are doing a good job is an important source of motivation.

RESEARCH SUMMARY

What do professionals gain from providing spiritual care?
To return to Narayanasamy, et al. (2002) for a moment, their work confirms that nurses
→

---

gained a sense of satisfaction from providing care that incorporated spirituality. They suggest that nurses who connected with the humanity of those that they cared for and developed positive working relationships with them also experienced a sense of healing and wholeness as their work progressed. There was satisfaction to be gained from providing holistic care that met the full range of their patients' needs. There was also a sense of reward gained from feedback received from users and carers who commented on the benefits accrued from this approach.

Comment

It would be unwise to extrapolate uncritically the above findings from nursing to social work as they are very different tasks. Nursing often involves more physical contact and intimate working with patients than social work. But what we can say is that providing users with a thoughtful, empowering, spiritually aware service which improves their lives can in itself be a motivating factor.

The next illustration I have chosen to use demonstrates that sometimes carers receive life long learning from their involvement with a cared-for person.

CASE STUDY

The teacher passes away

Peter W Hawkins is an Australian who writes from a Buddhist perspective. An integral part of his belief system is that all things are interrelated and interdependent. For a number of years he worked as a befriender for a man with learning disabilities called Stephen. Hawkins describes how he took Stephen on outings and visits and how over the years they developed a relationship that was mutually fulfilling and rewarding. On occasions, they met with hostility from people who felt that, due to his behaviour and appearance, Stephen should not be seen in public. On other occasions, Hawkins felt that his friend was let down by the services he received. In the final section of the story, Hawkins describes the last few days of Stephen's life on a hospital ward. He describes holding Stephen's hand and settling him down to sleep amid the busyness of the ward. He talks about the trust and friendship that had developed over the years and how much he had gained from befriending Stephen. He concludes with these poignant words:

> *My teacher had passed away. Without him, eleven years of learning and growth would not have been possible. The interbeing nature of our relationship was manifest right through to the end of his life, and I shall never forget it.*

> *(Adapted from Hawkins, 2004, pp53-4)*

Comment

Hawkins gives a view of a caring relationship/friendship which we are perhaps not familiar with. So often support or friendship offered to a disabled person by a non-disabled person is seen as being a one-way street where much is given but little is received in return. It is seen as an act of generosity or goodwill on the part of the able-bodied person, for which the disabled person should be grateful. I have overstated the case, and you may disagree, but I think that Hawkins's Buddhist background and his understanding of life positively shaped the way he viewed his relationship with Stephen.

To an extent, there are parallels with social work here. Traditionally, disabled service users have been seen as recipients who should be grateful for anything that they receive from the state. There has been an imbalance of power between them and social workers who have exercised considerable control over their lives. Social workers have always been gatekeepers for the state and often have had responsibility for allocating funding and resources.

C H A P T E R   S U M M A R Y

You may remember that one of the social work benchmark academic standards that I suggested we would explore at the beginning of the chapter talked about the social processes that lead to marginalisation, isolation and exclusion. We have done this by exploring a number of interrelated themes.

Starting with a brief overview of the ways in which disabled people have been viewed by society, I suggested that the spiritual needs of disabled people have been consistently disregarded, both by religious organisations and by professionals. This sits within the context of exclusion and oppression that often characterises the lives of disabled people.

We then used a case study to explore some of the issues around what could be described as spiritually aware social work practice. You were invited to think about your own developing understanding of spirituality and to consider the notion of organisational spirituality. The benefits of providing spiritually aware practice, both for service users and practitioners, were articulated.

Within adult care it could be argued that work with disabled people remains something of a Cinderella service, and that the literature on spirituality is relatively modest. In our next chapter, however, on social work with people with mental health problems, there is a considerable body of work on which to draw. Spirituality has been a significant driver in mental health for a number of years and mental health survivors have increasingly ensured that their spiritual needs are taken into account.

FURTHER READING

Johns, C (2000) Working with Alice: A reflection. *Complementary Therapies in Nursing and Midwifery*, 6, pp199–203.
This article describes the developing professional relationship between the author and a young woman who has a terminal illness. It provides a good example of reflective practice and accessibly states what the author gained from providing holistic/spiritual care.

Newell, C and Calder, A (2004) *Voices in disability and spirituality from the land down under. Outback to outfront.* Binghamton, NY: Haworth Press.
This is an excellent collection of articles from Australia which I have referred to on a number of times throughout the chapter. In particular, Chapter 9 by Elizabeth Mosely is well worth reading as it powerfully explores the exclusion that many disabled people experience.

WEBSITES

Disability Action: **www.disabilityaction.org.uk**.
An accessible website from a registered charity who work to promote the full inclusion of disabled people in all aspects of life, to lobby policy-makers and to change public perceptions of disabled people.

The National Centre for Independent Living: **www.ncil.org.uk**.
Contains lots of useful, accessible information regarding direct payments and independent budgets.

The University of Aberdeen Centre for Spirituality, Health and Disability: **www.abdn.ac.uk/cshad/**.
A useful resource for accessing more academic links and research.

Chapter 6

Working with spirituality: Mental distress

Introduction

No matter which area of social work you specialise in you will be working with people whose lives have been affected by mental illness. Children are not immune from the stresses and strains that can lead to mental distress. Young offenders often lead complex and fragmented lives sometimes exacerbated by mental health difficulties or substance misuse. Adults clearly experience periods of mental illness, including a disproportionate number of people with disabilities. In fact, all of us regardless of our position in life or age will either directly or indirectly have knowledge of mental distress. It is an often quoted statistic that one in four people at some point in their lives experiences mental illness and the baggage that can go with it – stigma, discrimination, social exclusion, poverty and isolation. Consequently, all social workers and other professionals who work with vulnerable people need to have an understanding of mental illness.

You may have noticed that I have already used a variety of terms to describe the experience we know as *mental illness.* This is deliberate as all terms which endeavour to describe the bewildering range of conditions and symptoms we collate together and know as mental illness are little more than abbreviations. Consequently, it is contested as to which description – *illness, difficulty* or *distress* – is the most appropriate. In the first part of this chapter we will briefly explore these terms and their validity. I will then introduce a different perspective by arguing that mental illness is as much a *spiritual crisis* as an illness. I will briefly expand this to other areas of social work practice as I would argue that many of the people that we work with are experiencing similar feelings of *spiritual dislocation.*

The main part of this chapter, however, will consider the social work task and how an understanding of spirituality is integral to the work that we do with people who are experiencing mental distress. We briefly revisit some themes we touched on earlier in the book, such as the importance of community and the formulaic approach to assessment which fails to capture the full person. I will also introduce a number of important issues such as the role of the mental health social worker, the developing notion of *spiritual assessment* and the importance of service user centrality. The chapter concludes by offering a brief outline of some of the limitations of spirituality.

The contested nature of mental illness

The predominant view within Western psychiatry is that there is an underlying physical, organic or biomedical cause to all mental health difficulties and therefore it is applicable to use the term *illness.* This powerful view sees little difference between a physical or a mental illness and is referred to as the *medical model.* Central to this understanding is the notion that mental illness can be assessed, diagnosed, treated and cured in much the same way as pneumonia or a stomach upset. While there are a number of flaws to this perspective, we need to acknowledge that some medical treatments and responses are highly effective and that this model does, and will, predominantly form the basis of psychiatric intervention in the United Kingdom.

Another way of interpreting the abnormal behaviour and unusual thoughts which characterise mental illness would be to view them as being a *difficulty*. While this is an ambiguous term, it infers that the behaviour or thoughts of the person are out of step with what could be considered to be normal and therefore pose difficulties both for society and the individual. The discipline of psychology suggests that such patterns of behaviour or cognition could have been learnt, or stem from, formative experiences and relationships in childhood, or from traumatic events which have adversely impacted on the person, or from fractured personal relationships and adverse social situations.

In contrast to these two models of understanding, the *social model* moves the discussion about the causes of *mental distress* away from the individual. While biological or medical causes are not dismissed, a distinct emphasis is placed on the role of social and environmental factors. Mental illness is not seen as being a matter of ill fortune or individual genetic weakness but as being caused or at least exacerbated by the social conditions and experiences of the person. *Distress* is a term sometimes used by social workers and survivors of the psychiatric system almost as a counterbalance to the dominance of the medical model with its emphasis on invasive clinical treatment and the management of symptoms. The word *distress* captures the unpredictability and bewilderment that often characterises the experience of mental illness. An accompanying emphasis on the social model allows for the discussion of such important dynamics as social exclusion, the misuse of power and the realities of oppression that can all lead to *distress*.

There are, of course, many explanations of what creates and sustains mental illness, and the three models I have offered are little more than caricatures that rarely operate in isolation from one another. A skilful practitioner needs to take into account all three models as working in complex situations with diverse needs requires a balanced view. Mentally distressed people rarely fit into neat categories and all three ways of understanding have something to offer.

ACTIVITY 6.1

Study the vignettes below and decide which model would be the most helpful in understanding the situation.

Chloe is an 18-year-old student who was involved in a serious road traffic accident twelve months ago in which her best friend was killed. The accident left her with an ongoing physical disability and her mobility is limited. She has flashbacks to the accident and is experiencing depression.

Leroy is a middle-aged man who has been unemployed and homeless for a number of years. He drinks heavily and has spent over twenty years in and out of the psychiatric system.

Shabnam has recently seen her GP, complaining of hearing voices that tell her to kill herself. The voices seem to be growing in intensity.

Comment

I suspect that you struggled to find one model that totally explained the given situation. At first sight, Chloe may well have post-traumatic stress disorder which could be alleviated by a psychological approach. On the other hand, her ongoing disability may be impacting on her and a social model approach which incorporates an analysis of social exclusion might be applicable. Leroy does not appear to have benefited from the treatment provided by the psychiatric system. His multiple social problems must be affecting his well-being and the social model may provide a helpful way forward. Equally, it seems unlikely that this approach by itself will be effective and other forms of intervention will be required. Shabnam requires a full psychiatric assessment. Depending on the result of that assessment, other interventions may be helpful. Crucially, we know nothing of her history or current circumstances, both of which may be of significance.

RESEARCH SUMMARY

Spirituality and psychiatry – crossing the divide
Andrew Powell (2007) is a doctor who describes his professional journey from being a traditional psychiatrist to practising transpersonal psychology – an alternative view of mental distress which fuses spirituality, psychiatry and elements of new age philosophy. Following his training in the 1960s he initially practised what we might call medical model psychiatry, but found that it lacked the ability to assist people in acute distress and was overly mechanistic in its approach. He eventually became disillusioned and began to raise questions about the validity of psychiatry.

> *The big questions about birth, life, death, what it is all for, why we must suffer, all those deep concerns that disquiet the troubled mind, generally have no place in which to find voice, and so don't get raised.*
>
> (Powell, 2007, p164)

In his search for an approach with a greater spiritual emphasis he subsequently embraced psychoanalysis and psychodrama, but felt that they, too, merely interpreted rather than explained the deep questions of life that troubled his patients. Powell was then introduced to healing and energy fields and began to explore and develop transpersonal psychology. Techniques include encouraging a patient to enter an altered state of consciousness, and spirit release where a spiritual entity which has attached itself to a patient is encouraged to leave. In many ways Powell's journey is remarkable both for its honesty and for the distance travelled. While some may raise questions about his destination, his emphasis on healing the underlying issues which create mental distress as opposed to merely treating the symptoms is of considerable merit.

Spiritual dislocation

All of the approaches and models we have discussed so far have something to offer and should not be dismissed. I would, however, like to suggest that mental illness can be seen to be as much a crisis arising from *spiritual dislocation* as it is a medical, psychological or social problem. So far, we have argued that spiritual understanding and the provision of spiritual care is essential for the provision of good social work practice. This is undoubtedly true, but I now want to extend that argument by suggesting that spirituality can give us a valuable insight into the causes of human distress.

Throughout this book I have argued that spirituality encapsulates a range of facets. It is about meaning, purpose, a sense of identity, a feeling of belonging, a sense of community, security, personhood and appreciation of life. Ultimately, all definitions fall short because what we are talking about is the human spirit – that unique, free-flowing gift that characterises and defines who we are.

But even taking my list of characteristics as a starting point, it is easy to see that many people who are labelled as mentally ill have little purpose or meaning in their lives, their sense of identity or understanding of who they are and where they fit into life is sometimes limited, their communities can be hostile towards them, they are more frightened than secure and their enjoyment of life is curtailed. You may think that this is an overly negative portrayal of mental illness and I would acknowledge that not all people in our psychiatric systems are characterised by these difficulties.

There is of course an argument that these problems are a direct result of being mentally ill. If you are unable to work due to mental illness it is likely that you will experience poverty. If your behaviour is erratic or alarming it is possible that family and friends will drift away. If you are in and out of hospital you may lose your tenancy and have difficulty establishing meaningful connections in your community. Due to your illness you may experience discrimination, stigma and labelling which leads to social exclusion. If you are on anti-psychotic medication or receiving invasive treatment such as electro-convulsive therapy it is possible that your self-confidence may be affected. All of these problems stem from the fact that you have a mental illness.

There is, however, an alternative view. I would argue that mental illness is a spiritual crisis brought about by a loss of, or dislocation from, those aspects of life which feed and reinforce the human spirit. On occasions, one single incident can lead to spiritual dislocation; for example, the death of a partner or family member, an accident or a traumatic event. Sometimes it can be a series of events which occur over a period of time such as childhood abuse or domestic violence. It may be that ongoing aspects of life such as poverty, unemployment, relationship difficulties, a lack of meaning and a lack of value being placed on your contribution gradually accumulate and lead to an inability to function. Fundamentally what is corroded by these events is the human spirit and our capacity to flourish as people. If we accept that what defines us as being human is the spirit within us, it follows that any damage to this spirit will naturally lead to an adverse reaction. That adverse reaction is what we label mental illness.

CASE STUDY

Councillor Manjula Paul Sood

Councillor Sood shared her life story at a 2006 Social Perspectives Network study day entitled Reaching the Spirit. *During her presentation she explained that she had emigrated to Leicester in 1970 and had led a very active life in politics and community work. She has received a number of prestigious awards for her contribution including a National Merit Award from the Prime Minister. She has also experienced several episodes of mental illness over a number of years.*

Her life story is characterised by a number of events which led to spiritual dislocation, for example, her experience of migration and the loss of ties of kinship and culture, her experiences of racism and discrimination and the hostility she faced as a new arrival to the country, and her struggle with illness and the untimely death of her husband, the last two of which potentially led to a loss of identity and well-being.

Councillor Sood describes her recovery from illness and her management of her life as having a clear spiritual element. Her personal faith is of importance to her as is a more general spirituality which she describes as an invisible force which holds her hand and moves her forward. While I would not wish to speak on her behalf there is an indication that the problems that caused her mental illness and the solution to her problems both had a spiritual component.

The full text is available from: www.spn.org.uk

Literature extract

Zohar and Marshall (2004), in their stimulating analysis of capitalism and business practice, take issue with Abraham Maslow's famous theory of a hierarchy of needs. You may remember that Maslow propounded that people have a number of needs which had to be sequentially met if they were to lead fulfilled lives. At the bottom of the pyramid are basic needs such as food and shelter, and at the apex is self-actualisation, that is, the need for personal meaning in life to be achieved and the opportunity for spiritual and psychological growth to occur. Zohar and Marshall argue that in wealthy, developed countries basic survival needs are routinely met and therefore Maslow's pyramid of needs should be inverted. They suggest that research conducted since Maslow's work in the 1950s has consistently shown that well-being depends on people reaching self-actualisation rather than purely having their basic needs met.

We know today that human beings are by definition creatures of meaning and value (that is, of self-actualisation). We need a sense of meaning and driving purpose in our lives. Without it we become ill or we die.

(Zohar and Marshall, 2004, p17)

While such statements should to be treated with an element of caution and we need to acknowledge that for many millions of people basic survival is perilous, they do support the notion that spiritual aspects of life are crucial for well-being.

To equate the experience of being mentally ill with spiritual crisis is not a new thought. Service users and professionals alike often associate the signs, symptoms and lived experience of mental distress with a loss of confidence, self-esteem and well-being – those mainstays of the human spirit. Others equally find that acute phases of mental illness lead them to question the religious faith that has guided and sustained them. For some, this *spiritual crisis* leads to a strengthening or renewal of faith while others may lose their faith. This loss is rarely recognised by busy professional staff and adds to the sense of spiritual dislocation.

Equally, the boundaries between spiritual experience and mental illness are blurred and inconsistent. Sacred texts and contemporary religions abound with visionaries, those who hear voices and those who claim to have insights from external powers. Crudely put, one person's prophet is another person's madman.

It may, however, be useful to consider how helpful the notions of *spiritual dislocation* and *spiritual crisis* are outside of the context of mental distress. For example, could it not be argued that the young person who is a user of the Youth Offending Service is also undergoing a spiritual crisis? It may be that they have experienced significant loss, disruption, rejection, bullying at school and peer pressure to offend. All of these life events corrode the human spirit and almost inevitably lead to a crisis. While it would be too mechanistic to suggest that all young people who experience these events offend, it could be argued that spirituality gives us an insight into the reasons why people may offend. Similarly, some drug users may have led unsatisfactory and chaotic lives leading them to use drugs as a form of release or self-medication. It is again possible that they came to a point of crisis where they were so dislocated from meaning, value and hope that drug use seemed to be a viable alternative. It would be inappropriate to speculate too much about the underlying reasons as to why people behave in the way that they do, as all people are unique and individual. All that I am proposing is that spirituality gives us an alternative insight into human behaviour which should not be disregarded.

Spiritual assessment

I now want to turn to some of the practice issues that arise for social workers who work in the field of mental health. As stated at the beginning of this chapter, while there are social workers who specialise in mental health, the issues of mental distress and their consequences impact on all aspects of our work.

As with many forms of social work, service users in mental health are used to being assessed, often by a range of professionals with a diversity of assessment tools. While policies such as the Care Programme Approach, introduced by the National Service Framework for Mental Health in the early 1990s, stipulated a need for a comprehensive multi-agency, multi-disciplinary approach to assessment there is one element which is consistently omitted from assessment: spirituality. More often than not, there is a tick box approach which touches on religion or faith, but offers little attempt to explore and understand and unpack spirituality as a driver of life and an essential source of hope, inspiration and purpose. One of the conundrums of contemporary social work is that social workers are expected to devise care packages to meet complex needs when they have little understanding of the real person they are working with. Acute phases of mental distress in particular often involve a sense of dislocation which naturally leads to a search for meaning. As Edwards and Gilbert (2007) record, service users want both recovery and discovery – they want to gain an understanding of their current situation and to use the insights gained to move forward.

Since 2003 NHS Boards in Scotland have been required by the Scottish Parliament to have a local plan in place to meet the spiritual needs of their patients and communities. Other (English and Welsh) NHS Trusts have followed suit and a number have well-developed spiritual care policies or plans. While these developments are welcome, there is still a danger that spiritual care is seen as being the sole responsibility of the chaplaincy service. In recent years, a number of policies and spiritual assessment tools have been devised which seek to address this need.

RESEARCH SUMMARY

The work of David Hodge: Developing a spiritual assessment toolbox
American social work academic David R Hodge has developed a number of different spiritual assessment techniques. He argues that spiritual assessment is an essential component of the social work task and that all social workers should have access to a toolbox of different assessment methods.

These include:

- **Oral spiritual history** *as the title infers this is where a service user is encouraged to tell their life story and to articulate their spiritual history.*

- **Spiritual lifemaps** *a pictorial account of a person's spiritual journey which speaks of their relationship over time with God or some other form of transcendence. Like a road map it records where a person has come from and where they are going.*

- **Spiritual genograms** *a diagrammatic representation of spirituality across a number of generations. The purpose is to produce a modified family tree which details significant spiritual interactions across time.*

- **Spiritual ecomap** *a snapshot of the immediate situation. A service user is encouraged to draw and describe their present relationship to potential spiritual assets such as friends and family.*

(Hodge, 2005, pp316–20)

While all of these techniques are useful I would want to sound a note of caution. As Benchmark Statement 4.6 reminds us, as social workers we need to recognise the macro factors that inform our task: the wider social, legal, economic, political and cultural context of people's lives. To this I would add the context of published research. As social workers we need to take into account the geographical and cultural context of research and make a judgement as to its applicability to our situation. Hodge writes from a viewpoint that reflects his cultural position: that of being an academic in a society with a strong Christian base where many people's lives are, at least superficially, influenced by faith and church attendance. His tools reflect that position and would need to be adapted to reflect the more secular nature of spirituality in Britain.

While I would encourage you to explore the work of Hodge and to use his tools, I suggest that the next more generic contribution is of more immediate use.

RESEARCH SUMMARY

A suggested model of spiritual assessment
Edwards and Gilbert (2007) review a number of models in their helpful study of spiritual assessment. By way of a summary they suggest that the following areas should be explored within a spiritual assessment.

- *Identity the components which contribute to the development of a person's core identity and how this identity may still be evolving.*

- *Beliefs and meaning those beliefs that give meaning and purpose to life and how these are reflected in practice.*

- *Sources of strength and hope derived from individuals, groups, places or experiences. Which sources are of crucial importance during times of crisis?*

- *Love and relatedness key relationships, both positive and negative. The role and influence of the family and a recognition of damaged relationships which may need healing.*

- *Vocation and obligation what sense of calling and obligation does the person have in their life?*

- *Affirmation does the person feel affirmed within their life, within their past and present experiences and relationships?*

- *Experience and emotion how has the experience of mental distress affected the meaning and understanding of life and how has this been emotionally expressed? How are negative feelings and emotions explored and handled by the person? How do the internal and the external worlds of the individual correspond and relate to one another?*

- *Courage and growth how has the person coped with previous crises and how adaptable are their views and beliefs?*

- *Transcendence how do people move beyond themselves and engage with a higher being or with their more intense outward emotions? This is not necessarily a religious matter but may relate to nature, art or sport – those exhilarating moments of life when we are taken beyond ourselves and our immediate, material lives.*

- *Rituals or practices a naming and analysis of the rituals that support understanding and life. They may be sacred or secular in nature.*

- *Community how does the person relate to their community? Do they experience their community as being hostile or beneficial?*

- *Authority or guidance where does the person go for guidance and authority at times of uncertainty or crisis where the meaning of life is insecure?*

Comment

Looking through this list of potential areas to explore in a spiritual assessment I felt that there was a number that required further exploration, for example *vocation and obligation.* Both of these old fashioned terms have religious overtones and may seem a little out of place in contemporary conversation. *Vocation* is relevant because it challenges us to name what our purpose in life is, what is our calling or destination. Many of you may have experienced a calling to enter social work or the caring professions. This calling will define your life path and will be a constant source of meaning and fulfilment. *Obligation* is again an unusual word and encourages us to question who we see as being the most important and enduring relationships in life. To whom do we feel obliged to offer time, support and assistance if required? Equally, who can we turn to at times of crisis, and who will feel that they are obliged to respond to us?

The list also talks about the importance of *transcendence.* We have alluded to the significance and importance of transcendence throughout the book and have suggested that healthy spirituality, of which it is a component, is a positive defence against the stresses of life. This is particularly relevant in the field of mental health, although we also need to recognise that sometimes connections with religious groups and beliefs can have an adverse effect on mental well-being. For example, Sims (2007) gives the example of a patient who developed severe depression and anxiety after being expelled from a Christian charismatic house church for her failure to end an inappropriate relationship. Previously her world, and her *vocation*, *obligations* and experience of *transcendence* had revolved around her membership of this group. Once it was taken from her she experienced a *spiritual crisis* which manifested itself in mental illness.

ACTIVITY 6.2

Consider the areas of life raised by the suggested spiritual assessment. If you were assessed by a social worker using this tool what would it reveal about you as a person and about your life? Do you think that you would be assessed as being spiritually healthy? Are there any aspects that you think have been omitted that should have been included?

Service user centrality

One of the main reasons why I think that spiritual assessment is of importance is that it emphasises the service users' lived experience and their understanding of their situation. Often social work assessments can be functional in nature concentrating on what a person can or cannot do. While it is important to know if a person can wash, dress and feed themselves it is equally important to tease out those areas of life which determine their spiritual well-being.

ACTIVITY 6.3

Make a list of the reasons why it is important to keep a service user central to their own assessment. Try and relate your ideas to what you have learnt about spirituality.

Comment

Service user involvement, encouraging service users to actively participate in their own assessment and care package configuration, is a given in contemporary social work. There is a danger, however, that it becomes little more than a mantra and that the reasons that underpin the concept are not articulated or explored. It is not appropriate to fully discuss service user participation, but I do want to say something about its importance to spirituality.

In particular, I want to suggest that if we keep the service user central to any assessment or intervention that we may undertake it ensures that we relate to the person and not to the illness. This may seem common sense, but there are plenty of anecdotes from our nursing colleagues about the cancer in bed four! Social work is equally guilty on occasions of concentrating on a presenting problem and not on the person with the problem. For example, I can remember being in allocation meetings where workers were given a choice of having a 'schizophrenic' or a 'depressive'. If we adopt this mentality we deny the uniqueness of the service user and run the risk of exacerbating the dislocation and crisis that first brought them to our attention. Powell (2007) in a similar vein talks about how some medical practitioners assume a position of authority and aloofness due to a lack of skill and a prevailing professional culture. They consequently fail to engage with the patient and miss an opportunity to kick start the process of recovery. They do not recognise that they are in the *position of being a fellow traveller on the unpredictable journey of life* (p162) and that mental distress is not only for others but could also be waiting for them around the corner.

Secondly, it may be that the contact you have with a service user is the first, and possibly only, opportunity they have ever had to explore the spiritual aspects of the crisis they are experiencing. It is possible that they need this time to disclose and explore a whole range of issues which impact both on their well-being and on their spirituality, for example areas of deep pain and uncertainty around loss, abuse, fractured relationships and past memories. If we are too preoccupied with forms and meeting deadlines and targets, this opportunity may be wasted. If, however, we are focusing on them and their understanding of their situation we will be aware of the opportunity and the deep privilege we have of *being a fellow traveller on the unpredictable journey of life.*

Social work and social inclusion

The phrase social exclusion, and the coterminous social inclusion, have received considerable attention over recent years. Concisely put, social exclusion is a pernicious process of polarisation and disadvantage that affects the poor and marginalised groups within society. It is characterised by a lack of opportunity, poverty, segregation and life restriction. In a vibrant capitalist economy where there are deep and widening divisions between those who succeed and those who do not, social exclusion has risen to the top of government agendas. While some excellent work has been done over the last few years in widening participation in education and leisure, and the advent of individual budgets has brought some creativity to care packages, many of the people you will work with in the psychiatric system will be socially excluded.

As previously discussed, exclusion, poverty, deprivation and marginalisation are all spiritually corrosive and adversely impact on the human spirit. As a social worker who has an awareness of the importance of spirituality, I would suggest that you have an important part to play in promoting social inclusion on two levels: the micro and the macro.

The social worker as integrator

Firstly, on a micro level you need to have an awareness of the spiritual importance of relationships, community ties and attachments. People cannot exist in a vacuum. They need to have a connection to other people, to feel rooted in groups and communities, and for their existence and contribution to be valued by others. We need to be careful not to make assumptions about people's lives, but many people with enduring or severe mental health problems do have poor connections and fractured relationships.

An important part of your role as a social worker will be to assist people to reintegrate back into their families and communities. This is especially crucial if they have had a number of hospital admissions which have led to relationships being put under pressure.

ACTIVITY 6.4

Consider the following case scenario

Alan is a divorced 45-year-old man who has a history of chronic depression. He lives alone in a three-bedroomed council flat and has two children aged eleven and nine who live near by. Alan has recently been very low in spirit and has been neglecting himself to such an extent that a voluntary admission to the local psychiatric unit was arranged. He has made good progress on the ward and after three weeks is ready for discharge. Unfortunately, during his admission his ex-wife has been in contact saying that his children no longer wish to see him as they have become embarrassed by his frequent admissions and odd behaviour. The local council are also trying to persuade Alan to move from his flat as they say he occupies a tenancy reserved for a family. They have offered him a maisonette on the fourth floor of a tower block some miles from his current address. During his stay it also comes to light that Alan's father, with whom he had regular contact, has recently died. Alan seems to have few friends or connections in the area and discloses that he often feels too frightened to leave his flat. Consequently, he has stopped attending the local bingo hall and snooker club which used to be his sole leisure activities.

ACTIVITY **6.4** *continued*

Make a list of the relationships and connections that need to be re-established or re-placed. What can you do as Alan's social worker to assist him to reintegrate back into the community?

Comment

I made the following list of relationships and connections that required attention.

- Alan's children do not live with him and no longer wish to see him.

- The local council are pressurising him to move away from his home and community. Potentially, he will lose a number of connections.

- Alan has no friends.

- He is too frightened to leave his flat. The reasons for this are unclear.

- Alan's father has died.

- He has stopped attending the bingo hall and the snooker club.

I am sure that you will agree that I have painted an accurate but rather grim picture of Alan's predicament. Given what we know about the importance of relationships and connection to spiritual well-being, there is a sizeable task to be undertaken. As a social worker with knowledge of the social model, anti-oppressive practice and the ability to work across boundaries, you are in an ideal position to support Alan.

Some of the issues may be relatively easy to address. For example, a direct payment would enable Alan to fund a care worker who could accompany him to the bingo hall and other leisure activities. This would get him out of the flat and would help to end his feelings of isolation. You may also need to approach the council on Alan's behalf regarding the accommodation issue. Depending on Alan's wishes, the council may have alternative accommodation within the same area or may drop their demand altogether.

The problem with Alan's children, however, is less straightforward. Often relationships can be put under strain where a person is in and out of hospital and where the family home is regularly visited by a succession of mental health professionals. Equally, some people find the stigma, labelling and behaviour that often accompany mental illness difficult to deal with. Working on the basis that his relationship with his children is of significance to him and them, there will have to be work done with all parties concerned to heal the rift. One way forward may be to encourage Alan and his children to meet on neutral ground or to seek the involvement of other family members to facilitate contact. Similarly, the death of his father is also a significant factor. Given his level of isolation and lack of positive relationships, the relationship with his father will be difficult to replace and it may be that it was a factor in Alan's admission to hospital. Either way, given the importance of healthy relationships to spiritual well-being, these losses need to be acknowledged and Alan needs to be supported to regain what he can from what he has lost.

I hope that you can see that this is essentially work with one person and one family. There are, however, related tasks which need to be done on a larger scale, what we might call social work on a macro level.

The social worker as an agent of social change

Social work has a proud history of working for social change and challenging oppressive structures in society. In the 1960s and 1970s in particular, social work contained a radical stream which sought to understand society in socialist terms and worked collaboratively with communities and groups to effect lasting change. Over the decades radicalism within social work has evolved and has manifested itself in several different guises, for example the emphasis on anti-racist practice in the 1980s. As we have previously discussed, community work and active participation in community affairs seems to have dropped off the agenda, although the National Occupational Standards for social work clearly encourage such involvement.

To return to our case study, I would suggest that there is a role for a social worker to be proactive in challenging some of the issues which are excluding Alan from active involvement in his community. For example, in collaboration with others, it might be possible to raise awareness of mental health issues on the estate. It might be possible to liaise with other community groups, such as schools and churches, to make facilities more available to excluded people. It may be possible to work in partnership with existing organisations who are seeking to encourage and facilitate community development – the creation of community and leisure facilities, pressure groups which work for change, groups who represent the estate to formal agencies such as the police and the council, etc. There may already be service user groups, such as Mind or Rethink, in existence that would value your support and expertise. While none of these activities are a panacea to social exclusion or mental illness they may be highly effective in reducing the stigma and exclusion that often characterise the experience of mental distress. After all, anything that makes a community a more vibrant, welcoming, active place to live is bound to have an impact on the well-being of those who live there.

In many ways the separation I have made between macro and micro social work is false as both are interconnected and are core tasks of social work. Social workers seek to facilitate positive change both in individuals and in communities. This notion is consistently reflected in the National Occupational Standards which state that social workers work with *individuals, families, carers, groups, communities.*

The notion of change is also embedded within the National Occupational Standards. For example, one standard that we highlighted at the commencement of this chapter challenges us to:

> *Apply and justify social work methods and models used to achieve change and development, and improve life opportunities.* (5.3)

The key words here are 'change', 'development' and 'improve life opportunities'. Good social work always seeks to promote growth and transformation.

These dual but connected aspects of the profession are summarised by the definition of social work adopted by the International Federation of Social Workers (IFSW):

> *The social work profession promotes social change, problem solving in human relationships and the empowerment and liberation of people to enhance well-being. Utilising theories of human behaviour and social systems, social work intervenes at the points where people interact with their environments. Principles of human rights and social justice are fundamental to social work.*

(Available from the IFSW website: www.ifsw.org)

ACTIVITY 6.5

Consider the definition of social work provided by the IFSW and the wording of National Occupational Standard 5.3. Think about a piece of work that you have recently done and tease out those aspects of it that were transformational in character. What social work methods and models did you use? What aspects of spirituality were present within the change you facilitated?

Comment

Sometimes if we are involved in process-driven formulaic social work it is not easy to tease out those aspects of work that promote change. Equally, social work is sometimes diffident about articulating those times when it has made a real difference to people and to communities. This is a task that you need to periodically return to and even use within supervision.

The limitations of spirituality in mental health social work

So far in this book I have provided a largely uncritical view of the role of spirituality. This is due to obvious reasons as I am trying to promote the value of spirituality and raise awareness of a spiritual approach among the social work profession.

We do need, however, to take a balanced view and recognise that in the field of mental health the religious views of some people, or how they are interpreted by others, can be a hindrance to their mental well-being. For example, some charismatic Christian groups interpret mental distress as being a punishment for sin and view a lack of healing as resulting from a lack of faith. Unsurprisingly, such views are often not helpful and only serve to reinforce the sense of dislocation and loss experienced by the service user.

There is also potential for an associated problem to occur. Sometimes these interpretations of the symptoms of mental distress can lead to a delay in formal assessment and treatment as religious leaders seek a cure through such events as exorcism and healing rituals and rites. Even worse, they may prevent the person ever receiving the help they need through an uncritical acceptance that community and religious leaders know best. You may recall that the enquiry into the circumstances surrounding the death of Victoria Climbié noted that church leaders had diagnosed her as being demon-possessed. While there was never a suggestion that Victoria was mentally ill, this assessment was one part of the jigsaw surrounding her abuse and prevented appropriate involvement from the statutory services. While there are many positive outcomes that derive from using spirituality we may need to reflect that it is not a catch-all cure. Often the best use of spirituality is where it is part of a wider understanding of mental illness, one which recognises both its importance and its limitations.

Finally, we also need to acknowledge that the struggle to find spiritual hope and the journey of spirituality can be intensely difficult, even painful. Nicholls (2007), speaking as a survivor of the psychiatric system, eloquently expresses this in her condemnation of superficial definitions of spirituality which leave out any notion of struggle or confusion.

> *Shallow versions of spirituality leave out the crucial truth that for many people their spirituality is intensely painful, harrowing, a source of torment and that for some it is a matter of life and death.*

(Nicholls, 2007, p105)

Nicholls borrows a term from a sixteenth-century Christian mystic called St John of the Cross who spoke of *the dark night of the soul* meaning a period of acute spiritual abandonment and desolation as a shorthand description of the type of limbo that people with mental distress can experience. She argues that sometimes the spiritual comforts of knowing who we are, where we have come from and where we are going to are unattainable for some, no matter how hard they may struggle.

C H A P T E R   S U M M A R Y

In this chapter I have touched on a number of issues relating to social work with mentally distressed service users. We initially discussed the different understandings of mental illness and suggested that the idea of *spiritual crisis* and *spiritual dislocation* were important conceptual tools. I then introduced the evolving concept of *spiritual assessment*. There is a considerable amount of work being undertaken on this important aspect of work and I am sure that you will be able to find journal articles and internet sites which will update your knowledge. I then mentioned a number of issues and ways of working, for example the crucial aspect of service user centrality and the connections between social work and social exclusion. We then looked at some of the many roles in mental health social work such as integration and promoting community development/change.

As an end piece I would encourage you to make links between the practice issues raised in this chapter and other areas of social work. For example, spiritual assessment should not be confined purely to people with mental distress as it has a much wider relevance. As mentioned in an earlier chapter, older people can experience loss and change in later life as being a *spiritual crisis*. What better way to assess these needs than by a spiritual assessment?

Equally, it is not just people with mental health problems who need to have social workers who are prepared to tackle unjust systems or to seek ways in which communities can be made better places in which to live. People with disabilities often experience similar pressures and exclusions where similar professional skills are required.

It is not purely mental health social work where we need to listen to service users and put their needs central to our work. This should be a primary focus of all our interventions, particularly when working with the most vulnerable where risk-taking has many complexities. In our next chapter we will be considering such a group, children, and looking at how spirituality can make a difference to their lives.

FURTHER READING

Butcher, H, Banks, S, Henderson, P and Robertson, J (2007) *Critical community practice*. Bristol: Policy Press.
This is a useful contemporary introduction to radical community work. Chapter 2, 'Power and empowerment: the foundations of critical community practice', by Hugh Butcher is especially helpful.

Coyte, ME, Gilbert, P and Nicholls, V (2007) *Spirituality, values and mental health: Jewels for the journey*. London. Jessica Kingsley
This is an excellent accessible compilation of essays and personal accounts of mental distress and spirituality.

Horner, N (2003) *What is social work? Context and perspectives*. Exeter: Learning Matters.
Chapter 2, 'The beginnings of social work: the comfort of strangers', offers a useful history of the profession, particularly the interconnection between the micro and macro tasks.

WEBSITES

The Royal College of Psychiatrists: **www.rcpsych.ac.uk**
This website contains the pages for the special interest group on spirituality and psychiatry. Their publications list and newsletter is a rich source of information on the changing interface between medicine and spirituality.

The Social Exclusion Task Force: **www.cabinetoffice.gov.uk**
The government established a Social Exclusion Unit in 1997 to tackle issues of deprivation and marginalisation. The Social Exclusion Task Force is its successor and seeks to embed issues of inclusion into key areas of government policy such as education and health. The website provides useful information about government initiatives and the ongoing need to tackle social exclusion.

Chapter 7

Working with spirituality: Children

5.1.1 Social work services, service users and carers.

- The social processes (associated with, for example, poverty, migration, unemployment, poor health, disablement, lack of education and other sources of disadvantage) that lead to marginalisation, isolation and exclusion, and their impact on the demand for social work services.
- The focus on outcomes, such as promoting the well-being of young people and their families, and promoting dignity, choice and independence for adults receiving services.

5.1.4 Social work theory.

- Research-based concepts and critical explanations from social work theory and other disciplines that contribute to the knowledge base of social work, including their distinctive epistemological status and application to practice.
- The relevance of sociological perspectives to understanding societal and structural influences on human behaviour at individual, group and community levels.
- The relevance of psychological, physical and physiological perspectives to understanding personal and social development and functioning.
- Social science theories explaining group and organisational behaviour, adaptation and change.

Introduction

In recent years there has been a significant increase in the level of interest and attention given to the spirituality of children. A plethora of books and articles has been written on the subject, and there is a well regarded *International Journal of Children's Spirituality*, all of which usefully explore issues and dilemmas. The focus has often been on educational and developmental issues, and we need to recognise that social work has been slow to acknowledge the importance of the subject.

To generalise, in past decades there has been an assumption that children do not possess fully formed spiritual lives or that their level of understanding is so limited that any reference to spirituality needed to be implicit or 'dumbed down'. While we clearly need to take into account a lack of intellectual development and maturity when working with children, it is an explicit message of this chapter that children recognise and express some complex spiritual ideas and have spiritual needs which social workers need to acknowledge.

In order to provide a framework for this chapter I want to pose and answer a number of questions. One of the questions I want to explore is the nature of children's spirituality and some of the difficulties there may be in enabling children to have and to express a spiritual life. An important consideration is that children and childhood are often viewed in an unhelpful stereotypical way. Following this discussion, we will briefly touch on issues which adversely affect spirituality – 'toxic childhood syndrome' and the ever present issue of child abuse. Both are relevant to an understanding of how life events can corrode the human spirit and cause long-term spiritual damage. I also want to allude to policy and legislation that is of importance to working with children. In particular, I want us to consider *Every Child Matters* (DfES, 2003) and use two outcomes as a framework for our later discussion. Finally, we will discuss some tools, storytelling, play therapy and life story work, which may help you to engage with children and spirituality. What I want you to gain from this chapter is an understanding that there are commonalities between children and adults and that our understanding and use of spirituality is no different. We are all engaged on a spiritual journey and children can offer valuable insights that aid our travel.

ACTIVITY 7.1

In order to help us begin to think about the themes of this chapter I would like you to consider the vignettes below and tease out the spiritual aspects of each case.

Ibrahim is an eight-year-old Palestinian boy who has entered Britain as an unaccompanied asylum seeker following the death of both his parents. He speaks English as a second language and is currently placed with foster parents.

Paula is twelve years old. She was systematically sexually abused by a neighbour for several years and has been admitted to hospital following an overdose of her mother's sleeping tablets.

Jonathan is a 14-year-old boy who is painfully shy and regarded by some as having learning difficulties. He is bullied at school and has been referred due to persistent school non-attendance.

Sarbjit is a 16-year-old girl who lives on the street with her mother who has long-standing mental health problems. Her mother has been in and out of psychiatric care for many years. Sarbjit has regularly been taken into care, but prefers living with her mother and persistently runs away if placed in foster care.

Comment

There are a number of spiritual aspects within these case studies. For example, there are common themes around loss, change, poor self-image and poor self-esteem. All of the children have problems connecting to family, peer group or community in some way. All of them have experienced challenges to their core identity and some have led transient lives where relationships have been difficult to make and sustain. There seems to be a lack of continuity in many of their lives and some have been abused, In other words their ability to cope with life has been adversely affected by a range of corrosive factors.

In recent years, the spiritual needs of children have received increasing recognition by academics and policy-makers alike. One reason for this has been a growing interest in what makes some children more resilient and more able to withstand the pressures and stress of life better than others.

RESEARCH SUMMARY

'Domains of resilience'
Daniel and Wassell (2002) identify six domains, or strengthening factors, which help children to withstand pressure or stress.

→

RESEARCH SUMMARY *continued*

Secure base:

- *Attachment relationship(s) – long-term resilience is linked to having developed a secure attachment to at least one person.*
- *Affection – physical contact that promotes warmth and love.*
- *Warm and sensitive parenting – appropriate to the individual needs of each child.*
- *Sense of self – a child valued by others will learn to value themselves. This differs from self-esteem in that it is located internally rather than linked to external achievement.*

Education:

- *Educational achievement is linked to resilience.*
- *School/pre-school attendance provides opportunities to boost resilience.*
- *Educational settings offer opportunities to develop other areas of resilience, such as friendships and social skills.*
- *Play provides opportunities to explore emotions, release tensions, and distract from problems.*

Friendships:

- *Good friendships in childhood can alleviate stress and provide strategies for coping.*
- *Social skills can be practised and enhanced.*
- *Children get more out of activities/experiences when friends are present.*
- *Secure attachments lead to stronger friendships.*

Talents and interests:

- *Self-esteem is central to resilience.*
- *Children with high self-esteem are realistic about their abilities and achievements.*
- *Children with low self-esteem are likely to attribute success to chance and expect to fail.*

Positive values:

- *Positivity towards self and others, e.g. being helpful, caring and responsible.*
- *Pro-social behaviours – knowing and using rules.*
- *Children learn from observing others.*
- *Messages from parents and carers about pro-social behaviours are more effective if they contain an emotional element.*
- *Empathy (behaviour/attitudes) can be enhanced through encouraging an awareness of the environment/nature, e.g. caring for pets.*

→

RESEARCH SUMMARY continued

Social competencies:

- *Autonomy (e.g. asserting own personality appropriately, healthy separation from carer, having a go at doing tasks).*

- *Self-control (e.g. ability to wait, turn-taking).*

- *Temperament (e.g. normally cheerful, enjoys humour, can be comforted).*

Comment

To return to our vignettes for a moment, I am sure that you can see that many of the children lack the strengthening factors identified by Daniel and Wassell (2002). The domains clearly contain spiritual components: the development of self-esteem, the importance of friendship, attachment and so on. There are also connections to recent children's legislation which we will consider shortly.

With those thoughts still fresh in your mind, I want to encourage you to engage with a number of questions which will help us tease out the spirituality of children and its relevance to social work.

Are children innately spiritual?

I have already made the argument in this book that all people are spiritual and that spirituality is an essential component of what it is to be human. Consequently, it should not be a surprise to learn that children, too, commonly express spiritual ideas and thoughts and that spirituality is of significance to them.

A number of authors, however, go further and suggest that children are innately spiritual, that is spirituality is part of their make-up, it is a naturally occurring feature of their lives. For example, Hay and Nye (2006), who conducted a three-year study of children's spirituality in England, concluded that children possessed an 'implicit spiritual discourse'. The children in their research cohort were able to reflect on and talk about profound questions of life and death and how they connected to themselves and to others in a sensitive and coherent way. Some children used religious terminology or metaphors to express themselves, while others did not. However they chose to express themselves, it was clear that their level of understanding of complex spiritual issues was considerable.

The spiritual world of children

Tobin Hart (2003) argues that children possess vibrant spiritual lives even prior to the development of formal reasoning. Through his research Hart identified five spiritual capacities which channel and characterise the spiritual development of children. These are:

→

- *Wisdom* knowledge which comes from being open in heart and mind. While wisdom is often assumed to come from maturity and years of life experience, Hart argues that children are naturally open to spirituality and sometimes possess intuitive insights not accessible to adults.

- *Wonder/awe* the way in which the child explores and experiences the joy and mystery of the world around him/her.

- *The relationship between self and others* the development and understanding of relationships between the child and other people, or groups of people, or the external world. As part of this development Hart suggests that even young children have a capacity to feel care and compassion towards others. This may be to other children in distress, or to pets and animals. This notion is interesting as it seems to suggest that children are innately caring and tender towards others. In other words, they have a natural capacity to exhibit one of the core features of spirituality. It also contradicts the perceived wisdom of many psychology theorists who argue that children are self-centred and egotistical.

- *Wondering* Hart argues that children are natural philosophers who instinctively seek to explore the profound questions of life.

- *Seeing the invisible* the awareness that some children have of what could be loosely referred to as psychic phenomena, such as ghosts, apparitions or psychic lights. Hart is cautious about the way that some adults overemphasise these abilities and suggests that intellectual and emotional development is of greater importance.

Comment

It is perhaps a matter of debate as to how spiritually aware children are and at what age they become capable of understanding the complexities of life and death. It would be unwise to make sweeping assumptions about ability or level of understanding as all children are different and live their lives in very different family and cultural contexts. What we can say is that spirituality and the discussion of spiritual topics should not be considered to be purely the privilege of the adult.

Do children talk about their spiritual experiences?

Despite this renewed emphasis on children and their spirituality and an acceptance that children do have spiritual lives, it is not to say that children find it any easier than adults to talk about spirituality. Hyde (2008), in his study of the spirituality of Australian children, identified two factors that affected the ability of children to talk about spirituality. The first factor was what he terms 'material pursuit'. Unsurprisingly, living in a capitalist society founded on the notion that money brings happiness, the children in Hyde's study believed that what was most important in life was the acquisition of wealth. Possessions were of more importance than people, and a good life centred on going to McDonald's and buying the latest consumer goods. Secondly, Hyde found that children actively avoided talking about issues of meaning and value in life and felt positively uncomfortable if pressed to do so. One tactic they used was to trivialise the discussion and to change the subject away from spirituality onto more mundane issues.

Not for the last time in this chapter, we might reflect that children are no different to adults. When adults cannot fully understand or articulate an issue they change the topic of conversation or seek to hide their inadequacy through discussion of a less challenging subject. Consequently, as one of my more perceptive students recently suggested, spirituality has joined religion and politics as a conversational no-go area.

This reluctance has been described as a suspicion of the spiritual which effectively amounts to a taboo in society (Hay, 1985). This taboo is strong and potentially has the ability to discourage or nullify the development of spiritual awareness. For example, Scott (2004) accumulated over twenty adult recollections of spiritual experiences which had occurred in childhood. Although these spiritual experiences, typically dreams, were of some significance the adults disclosed that this was the first time many of them had felt comfortable in talking about them. As children they did not feel able to discuss their experiences with friends because they were frightened that they would be seen as strange or foolish. Equally, they did not feel able to talk to their parents because they recognised the taboo surrounding spirituality at an early age. Scott argues that this silence leads to a 'cycle of secrecy'. Children do not feel able to talk to adults, adults are therefore not aware of the spiritual lives of their children and do not initiate discussion. Children then grow into adults and the cycle of silence and disregard is perpetuated.

ACTIVITY 7.2

Think back to your childhood. Did you have spiritual experiences such as dreams and premonitions or see unusual things that you did not feel able to disclose to either your friends or family? If so, why do you think that you were not able to freely talk about your experiences?

Comment

You may have come from an overtly religious background where it was natural, even encouraged, for you to share spiritual insights and experiences. It could be that you attended a faith school where friends were 'on the same wavelength' and did not feel embarrassed or bemused talking about spiritual experiences. Conversely, it may have been very difficult for you to acknowledge spiritual occurrences. Living as we do in a society dominated by science and rationalism we may reflect that it could become even more difficult for our children to openly discuss their spirituality.

Another potential difficulty is that children are sometimes viewed in unhelpful, stereotypical ways which allow adults to ignore their insights. The following research identifies some of these stereotypes in relation to children and spirituality.

RESEARCH SUMMARY

Mercer (2006) identifies a number of stereotypical images of children which she has drawn from the Christian tradition and from her academic work. The images include the following:

- *The child as a mystic   This reflects some of our previous discussions where children were clearly in touch with spiritual ideas and experiences. Mercer brings to mind the famous observation made by psychoanalyst Carl Jung that children's lives touch holiness. They often seem to have connections with mystery and are able to articulate mystical experiences. There is a danger that these experiences are ignored as being a passing phase deriving from an over-active imagination.*

- *The child as a sage   The child is seen to possess knowledge beyond their years. Mercer gives the example of a five-year-old child she observed comforting a bereaved older woman in a church congregation who had been ignored by the adults around her. The child naturally empathised with the woman and found it easy to connect to her sense of loss.*

- *The child as a holy fool   Where children utter words of wisdom which are often seen as amusing or charming, or as stemming from a lack of worldly understanding. Mercer gives the example of a child who, when asked where her hair came from, replied that it came from God. This remark led to laughter and teasing, although it was a credible attempt to answer one of life's mysteries which could not have been bettered by many adults.*

Comment

It is interesting that this list contains a number of similarities with the stereotypes of people with learning disabilities that we mentioned in Chapter 5 and with the work of Hart (2003) cited above. We might reflect that sometimes there is a danger that the insights of adults onto the world of children can be simplistic and subjective. As always, we need to maintain a balanced perspective that neither overstates nor dismisses the validity of these expressions of spirituality.

In social work and other professional fields such as education, there is an increasing emphasis placed on listening to the voice of children and encouraging expression and creativity. As Hay and Nye (2006) argue there is a need for educationalists, practitioners and parents to release the understanding and creativity of children rather than constrict their thoughts to questions which have straightforward answers. Sometimes questions about life and death, to which none of us have a straightforward answer, are the most fertile and exciting to explore.

What factors adversely affect children's spirituality?

The straightforward answer to the question is that the same factors which cause adults to lead spiritually impoverished lives similarly corrode the lives of children. For example, the experience of social exclusion, poverty, the breakdown of significant relationships and living in a fractured community can lead to spiritual dislocation for adults and children alike. There are, however, discrete pressures on children which we need to note.

Toxic childhood syndrome

Palmer (2007) neatly encapsulates the problems children face growing up in contemporary Britain through her use of the phrase 'toxic childhood syndrome'. On the one hand, children have ready access to more opportunities, money, fast-food outlets and electronic gadgets than at any time in the past. These benefits derive from living in a fast-moving, wealthy, consumer society and arguably provide a high quality of life. Conversely the downside of these riches – junk food, violent video games, broken family relationships and parents who work long hours and are cash rich but time poor – can lead to an impoverished childhood.

What children sometimes seem to lack is a sense of being loved and valued purely for who they are, those emotional and spiritual affirmations, which clearly correspond to the 'domains of resilience' which we discussed earlier and which are essential to developing a sense of identity and well-being. They sometimes lack family life which gives them time and space and permission to explore, develop and grow from children into adulthood. Consequently, they are required to have a robust sense of self and the ability to draw on their own inner spiritual resources from a young age. Some children are able to do this, others are not.

Comment

As social workers we need to be mindful of the pressures faced by children growing up in a fragmented, competitive society where it seems increasingly difficult for children to be safe and secure and enjoy the innocence and freedom of being children. Neither should we fall into the trap of being misty eyed about childhood. There have always been dangers and challenges associated with being a child.

Child abuse – the crushing of the spirit

One of the dangers of being a child is that you could be abused physically, sexually, emotionally or in a combination of ways, by those adults who are supposed to be caring for you. In the aftermath of the Baby Peter scandal in 2008 Christine Gilbert, the chief executive of Ofsted, the inspectorate for children's services, told the House of Commons Select Committee on Children, Schools and Families that three children a week – a total of 210 – died in England and Wales as a result of abuse between April 2007 and August 2008 (Gilbert, 2008). Similarly, NSPCC research extrapolates that there could be as many as 1.4 million children in Britain who regularly experience emotional abuse, are humiliated, shouted at and made to feel worthless (NSPCC, 2006). These figures are shocking and indicate that much needs to be done to make Britain a safer place for children. Equally, we need to recognise the work undertaken by social workers and others to protect children in Britain which actually has a good record in terms of a low rate of child deaths.

Many of you reading this book will either work in children's services or have an aspiration to do so, and will be all too familiar with the difficult lives that a minority of our children live. It may seem simplistic to suggest that one of the consequences of child abuse is that the spirit of the child is systematically crushed and that spiritual development is adversely affected. Margaret Crompton (2001) notes a number of examples provided by practitioners of ways in which children are crushed or 'dis-spirited' by their abusive experiences. One case she cites is of a young girl who was unloved and unwanted by her family. Consequently, she spent most of her time trying to gain their attention and was described as being unsmiling, lifeless and 'without spirit'. Another social worker describes how she sees abused children as being dragged down by their painful experiences. Their natural exuberance for life is crushed and their slumping body language is indicative of the hurt they experience.

Some may argue that the spiritual damage caused by abuse or neglect is of no great importance compared to the other more obvious long-term damage sustained by abused children. I would, however, suggest that the impact on those crucial areas of spiritual growth, such as developing a robust sense of identity and a sense of self, the growth of personal confidence and a measure of emotional and mental well-being, can lead to significant difficulties in the future.

Religious belief and child abuse

It is also relevant to note that sometimes the religious beliefs of parents or carers can increase the risk of abuse to children in their care. As we have previously noted, a feature of the Victoria Climbié case was the belief of her carer, her great-aunt Marie-Therese Kouao, that Victoria was demon-possessed (Laming, 2003). Victoria was taken to a number of predominantly African churches in London where advice was sought as to how her behaviour might be improved by exorcism. It is unclear whether this was a smokescreen by the great-aunt or a genuine belief that such help was required. Either way, it was concerning to the Laming inquiry that no one within the church leadership questioned the great-aunt or actively assisted Victoria in the last few weeks of her life.

RESEARCH SUMMARY

Following the Climbié inquiry and other cases of child abuse where demonic possession was cited as a factor, the Department for Education and Skills (DfES) commissioned a piece of research entitled Child Abuse Linked to Accusations of Possession and Witchcraft. *This is what they found:*

- *From January 2000 to mid-2005 they identified 38 cases involving 47 children where children had been accused of being evil, of being possessed by spirits or of having connections with witchcraft.*

- *Half of the children had been born in the UK, half were from Africa.*

→

RESEARCH SUMMARY *continued*

- *Boys and girls were equally at risk.*
- *School teachers were particularly important in identifying the signs of abuse – tiredness, disengagement, a lack of food, poor clothing, poor attendance, etc.*
- *The majority of cases came from London, but cases in other areas of England were also identified.*
- *Children identified by their carers as being possessed exhibited a range of behaviours. These included bed wetting, physical or learning disabilities, nightmares and challenging behaviour.*
- *The children were abused in a range of ways, often in an attempt to rid them of their evil spirit. Cures ranged from enforced fasting, sleeping in the bath, beating, burning, cutting and the threat of abandonment.*
- *In terms of outcomes, 18 children were placed in foster care, 2 were placed in secure care, 7 returned home but were placed on the child protection register and 10 went overseas. The fate of the latter is unknown.*

(Stobart, 2006)

These connections between belief and child abuse are not new and we need to be clear that they are often used solely to justify the actions of abusive adults. In the 1980s there was considerable debate about the extent of 'ritual abuse' where perpetrators supposedly sacrificed children or used children in elaborate satanic rituals. The most famous case involved a number of children from the same extended family on the Broxtowe estate in Nottingham. Various allegations about ritualised abuse were made and were enthusiastically explored by the press and childcare experts. A number of formal inquiries followed the successful prosecution of those adults responsible for the abuse, including a joint police/county council investigation. The inquiries categorically disproved any connection between the abusive behaviour of the adults and Satanism (Robinson, 1999).

ACTIVITY **7.3**

At the beginning of this chapter I asked you to consider several vignettes and to identify the spiritual aspects of those cases. Having progressed a little further into the chapter I would like to invite you to reconsider two of the case scenarios and think about the long-term spiritual consequences for Paula and Sarbjit.

Paula is twelve years old. She was systematically sexually abused by a neighbour for several years and has been admitted to hospital following an overdose of her mother's sleeping tablets.

Sarbjit is a 16-year-old girl who lives on the street with her mother who has long-standing mental health problems. Her mother has been in and out of psychiatric care for many years. Sarbjit has regularly been taken into care, but prefers living with her mother and persistently runs away if placed in foster care.

Comment

Paula's life already seems to be unravelling. From what we know about the consequences of sexual abuse, it is probable that she will have feelings of powerlessness, low self-esteem and the inability to form positive relationships. The long-term spiritual consequences could be that her sense of value, self-worth and identity are impaired. Equally, she may be vulnerable to mental health problems.

Sarbjit seems to have little permanency or stability in her life. There could be issues around the development of her identity and there seems a strong possibility that she is missing out on her childhood which is being replaced by disjointed care arrangements and the need to look after her mother. She may have purpose in her life, supporting her mother, but leads a dysfunctional existence where her own needs are not being appropriately met. The long-term spiritual consequences could be that she finds it difficult to form relationships or to make connections with others.

These suggestions are conjecture and we need to be careful not to be deterministic about the lives of damaged children. Nonetheless, to borrow some of the terminology used by Crompton (2001), these children are almost certain to be 'without spirit' and 'dis-spirited', and there will be long-term implications for them if appropriate support is not provided.

Legislation and spirituality

Despite the increasing prominence of spirituality and the emphasis placed by successive governments on holistic assessment and interventions, social care legislation rarely explicitly mentions spirituality and spiritual need. This is broadly the case for childcare legislation which has consistently promoted the requirement for social workers and other childcare professionals to recognise and protect the religious and cultural needs of children as distinct from the spiritual needs of children. For example, the Children Act 1989 (section 31) stipulates that a child who is subject to a care order must be brought up in the religious faith they already possess. You may feel that the distinction I am making between the inclusion of religion and the non-inclusion of spirituality is a fine one and that the wording of legislation and policy is not too important as long as the outcome is positive. I would accept that this is a legitimate argument but would also suggest that the terms religion or culture need no longer adequately reflect the plurality and complexity of belief and spiritual practice in contemporary society.

On occasions, neither religious nor spiritual needs are recognised. For example, the policy initiatives deriving from the *Every Child Matters* Green Paper (DfES, 2003) sought to improve the lives of children across the health, social care, voluntary and education sectors by identifying five critical domains:

- *Be healthy* the promotion of the physical, emotional and sexual health of children including the adoption of a healthier lifestyle.

- *Stay safe* protection from maltreatment, neglect, harm, bullying and accidental harm.

- *Enjoy and achieve*   the promotion of attendance, enjoyment and achievement at school.

- *Make a positive contribution*   the development of engagement in society and community, the promotion of positive and responsible behaviour.

- *Achieve economic well-being*   the encouragement and opportunity to access further education, employment or training after leaving school. The wherewithal to live in good homes and enjoy material goods and transport systems.

Every Child Matters includes an Outcomes framework which details how these goals can be met and how outcomes can be improved for children (DfES, 2005). Interestingly, given the all-embracing and aspirational nature of the framework, the religious/spiritual needs of children are not mentioned. It could be argued that these needs are implicitly acknowledged and we will examine the practice implications of this a little later. *Every Child Matters* and the legislation that followed, the Children Act 2004, were policy responses to a number of drivers – not least the inquiry into the death of Victoria Climbié by Lord Laming, and the United Nations Convention on the Rights of the Child which was formulated in 1989.

Interestingly, the Convention does include reference to the spiritual needs of children. For example, Article 14 requires that *States [and] Parties shall respect the right of the child to freedom of thought, conscience and religion.* Every child shall have *Freedom to manifest one's religion or beliefs … subject only to such limitations as are pre-scribed by law and are necessary to protect public safety, order, health or morals, or the fundamental rights and freedoms of others* (Office of the United Nations High Commissioner for Human Rights, 1989). Other sections of the Convention are equally explicit and it is disappointing that children's legislation in Britain does not always reflect this position.

There are, however, commonalities between the outcomes and aspirations of *Every Child Matters*, the UN Convention and other more prominent rights legislation such as the Human Rights Act 1998. While there may be an element of disappointment at the overall lack of an explicit recognition of spirituality, there is more interest now than at any time in the past.

I now want to use two of the outcomes at the heart of *Every Child Matters* as a broad guide to our discussion of practice issues.

Be healthy

This set of aims and outcomes promotes healthy living and has a particular emphasis on being mentally and emotionally healthy. While these terms may be contested I do not want to enter into a debate around nuances and definitions. What I do want to do is to remind you of some of the previous content of the book and again make a connection between spiritual expression in adulthood and childhood. Social workers often meet children who have been significantly damaged by their experiences. Part of their vulnerability is that they are mentally and emotionally 'unhealthy'. While there may be a range of people and professionals who will subsequently work with them, often the social worker will have a pivotal role in exploring and addressing the pain of the child.

This is clearly a highly skilful and professional task which should not be undertaken lightly. Many organisations will have clear policies and procedures which explicitly state who may undertake this work and how they will go about it, but there will often be room for creativity in your approach. For example, you may remember that earlier in this book we talked about the role of the arts and how singing and creative activity could promote confidence and a sense of well-being.

Crompton (2001) provides a number of examples where children have used music to express their feelings of anger and a sense of loss. She recalls one poignant example where she had the privilege of connecting with a damaged child through the sharing of music.

Literature extract

Laurel [and I...] were in the sitting room of a secure unit. I had regarded her as a 'very naughty girl' of whom I felt some fear and with whom I expected little communication. However, unexpectedly marooned together, we both, for different reasons, felt spare, anxious and awkward. I no longer saw her as a 'very naughty girl'. She huddled on the settee, playing and re-playing one record, very wistful and wailing. The music expressed the lost girl who used it to create a sound environment, to fill up silence, maybe to control our conversation, but principally to communicate how she felt. We had only a brief time together and did not expect to meet again. But we made some contact, enabling me to meet a real girl instead of the imagined monster. In the dining room, back with her peers, Laurel became brash, notice-me-but-hold-off again. The music and her freedom to choose, play and listen to it had helped her to drop her tough veneer, even if only for a few minutes. In our brief music enabled contact, both the lost girl and I gained some spiritual nurture.

(Crompton, 2001, p59)

Comment

It would be facile to suggest that this shared experience was some sort of therapeutic breakthrough but it allowed adult and child to connect at a level which was previously not possible. The child expressed herself in a way that she probably could not have done if asked to use language. For a moment or two, an adult was able to sense the pain and confusion of the child. And as always, the sharing of pain and gaining an insight into the spirit of another person is a profound and moving experience.

Crompton also suggests that periods of silence and reflection can be healing. Sometimes the lives of children (and practitioners) are so full of noise and busyness that taking time out simply to sit with a child can be very healing.

Think about a child you have worked with who has been hurt or damaged in some way. What techniques or skills did you use to 'get alongside them' – to understand their world and assist them to articulate their experiences? Did any of them have a spiritual basis?

Comment

I suspect that those of you who are experienced practitioners were able to provide a list of methods and techniques that you have used. For those of you who are less experienced, I would argue that many commonly used skills and techniques have a spiritual basis.

Life story work seeks to piece together the often fractured life of the child through the collation of important artefacts, memories and paperwork such as birth certificates, letters and photographs. Valuing the life of a child and encouraging them to piece together their identity and to discover what has made them who they are has a powerful spiritual basis. For all of us need to know who we are. All of us need to have a sense of personhood and an understanding of those parts of our existence, however painful, which have moulded us into the people we have become.

Play therapy is another obvious example. Like life story work, play therapy is a specialist activity which should not be undertaken by the untrained practitioner. It employs a range of different tools and techniques including dance and movement, sand play, drama, art and puppetry and is based on a number of clear principles and therapeutic outcomes. At its heart, however, is an understanding that play is a natural activity which is essential for the healthy development of body and mind. Play therapy can be used to tackle a range of emotional and psychological difficulties and has a clear spiritual basis. It recognises the validity of the world of the child and seeks to offer a measure of healing via a medium which is accessible to every child, however limited or damaged they may be.

Storytelling is one of the techniques some of you may have included that you use to engage with children and young people. In some cultures the spoken word and the passing on of histories and stories in an oral form is of equal, or more, importance than the written word. This is particularly the case in African, African-Caribbean and Middle Eastern cultures where the spoken word has been portable across the world and secure in the minds and hearts of people on the move. You may remember in Chapter 4 on older people we briefly spoke about Black Elders and the importance of the oral tradition. Stories of course do not always come in oral form and not all children find stories accessible or helpful. On the contrary, stories traditionally fulfil a number of functions and may be stereotypical, frightening or even oppressive. Consequently, care needs to be taken if storytelling is to be utilised.

RESEARCH SUMMARY

Crompton (2001) in her helpful guide on children's spirituality highlights the fact that many of the stories from the world's religious traditions explore themes which might have especial significance for children in the social care system. For example:

Adoption/fostering/step-parent

- *a child cannot be cared for by its own parents and is looked after by other adults who are kind and caring – Krishna (Hinduism), Moses (Judaism, Christianity, Islam);*

- *an adopted/fostered child becomes successful and is not disadvantaged by being cared for outside of its birth family – Esther (Judaism, Christianity), Krishna (Hinduism), Moses (Judaism, Christianity, Islam), Muhammad (Islam).*

Single parenthood

- *an unmarried girl conceives and faces public humiliation and family rejection – Mary (Christianity, Islam).*

Separation and loss

- *birth parents are dead – Esther (Judaism, Christianity), Muhammad (Islam);*

- *birth parents are unable to care for their child due to living in dangerous times – Krishna (Hinduism), Moses (Judaism, Christianity, Islam);*

- *parents separated – King Solomon and the Queen of Sheba (Rastafarianism, Judaism, Christianity, Islam).*

Comment

It is interesting that so many of the stories from religious tradition explore the difficulties of life. Perhaps they serve to remind us that human frailty has changed little over the millennia. At the heart of storytelling is a spiritual dynamic as stories enable us to reach beyond ourselves and to seek explanations for a world which is sometimes messy and difficult. They allow us to tap into the spiritual pain or uncertainty of others and to share our common humanity. They facilitate communication and healing in a way that is often not possible using other methods.

Achieve economic well-being

The overall tenure of this *Every Child Matters* outcome is for children to enjoy and make the most of their educational opportunities, and then use these opportunities as a springboard into employment. With employment comes fulfilment and reward enabling young people to responsibly enjoy wealth and material possessions. I am sure that many social workers will recognise that for some of the children and young people we work with the path I have described is at best problematical and for many simply unobtainable. We know, for example, that the educational and employment outcomes for children in the care system do not compare favourably with children who are not in public care.

RESEARCH SUMMARY

Care Matters: Transforming the lives of children and young people in care

This Green Paper published by the DfES in 2006 represents a co-ordinated government response to the growing discrepancy in educational and employment outcomes between children in public care and their peers. It proposed a number of radical solutions including the strengthening of the corporate parenting role of local authorities. The paper highlighted a number of depressing statistics:

- GCSE attainment for children in care is not only far behind that of all children, but also significantly lower than that of children entitled to free school meals and those from deprived communities. Even when compared against children with similar levels of special educational needs, deprivation and mobility, children in care do significantly worse. Out of school, they often fare poorly and are three times more likely to be cautioned or convicted of an offence than other children.

- The gap between children in care and other children gaining 5A*–C grades has not narrowed but has begun to widen.

- At the age of 19, only 19 per cent of care leavers are in further education and 6 per cent in higher education, compared to 38 per cent of all young people participating in one or the other.

- Young women aged 15 to 17 who have been in care are three times more likely to become teenage mothers than others of their age.

- Research suggests that around 27 per cent of adult prisoners have spent time in care.

- Over 30 per cent of care leavers are not in education, employment or training at the age of 19 compared to 13 per cent of all young people.

(DfES, 2006)

Comment

In the Foreword to the Green Paper, Alan Johnson, the then Secretary of State for Education and Skills, stated that:

> Some may say that part of the reason for this [underachievement] is that children who enter care come disproportionately from poor backgrounds and have complex needs, but it is inexcusable and shameful that the care system seems all too often to reinforce this early disadvantage, rather than helping children to successfully overcome it.

(DfES, 2006, p6)

As social workers we need to be balanced in our appraisal of the care system and recognise the validity of such criticism. While the statistics I have used are damning we should not forget that many children entering the care system come from damaged family backgrounds where educational achievement is afforded little priority. The care system works well for many of these children providing them with opportunities that they would not otherwise have had. As we have explored in this chapter, many children live lives characterised by a poverty of mind, spirit and relationships.

As a final thought I want to encourage you to evaluate and value the role of social work when working with children.

Confronting inequality: A moral and spiritual task

Throughout this book I have consistently drawn your attention to issues of oppression and ways in which social workers need to incorporate an anti-oppressive stance into their work. What we have not done is to make clear that social work is, or should be, a moral activity where individual social workers make decisions based on sound ethical judgements. For example, it may be that there are sufficient concerns about a particular child that would enable proceedings to commence to remove that child from its family. A social worker not only has to make a range of procedural and legal decisions but also has to make a moral judgement – is removal in the best interests of the child. In other words, is it a *good* thing to do? Is it the *right* decision based on the evidence I have before me? These decisions are always difficult to make and there is a truth in the adage that social workers are damned if they do and damned if they don't.

Part of the moral fabric of social work is that practitioners recognise that we do not live in an equal world where all people are given the same opportunities. Those of you already in practice will know the realities of working with children who have suffered racism, ageism, disablism and other forms of structural oppression. Confronting these inequalities is never going to be easy and you may think that as an individual there is little that you can achieve.

On the contrary, I would suggest that you are working in an anti-oppressive way every time you:

- advocate for a family to receive the correct amount of welfare benefit payment or to gain appropriate housing;

- support an asylum-seeking family to have their views heard;

- protect a woman and her children from domestic violence;

- protect a child from abuse, bullying or harassment;

- argue against the labelling, discrimination and stigma that blights the lives of so many of our children;

- work with young people leaving the care system and ensure that they have the same level of support and resource that others have;

- support young offenders through the criminal justice system and seek to understand what causes them to offend.

What is important, however, is that you gain an understanding of why you seek to work in this way. It may well be that organisational policies, professional values and codes of conduct encourage you to do so, but essentially you are driven by a shared humanity and an understanding that the misuse of power is wrong. To adopt briefly a religious metaphor, the struggle we have against powerful forces which are deeply embedded in our society can be seen as a fight against evil. While not all of you may be comfortable using this term, it usefully highlights the spiritual context of social work practice.

C H A P T E R   S U M M A R Y

In this chapter you have examined a number of issues relevant to children and spirituality. You started by exploring the reasons why there has been an increased awareness of the spirituality of children in recent years, for example concerns around resilience, and looked at some of the research which explores the spiritual world of the child. After acknowledging that children do have a vibrant spirituality you then looked at some of the difficulties and taboos that may inhibit their ability to be open about their experiences. Part of the problem is that children are sometimes viewed in stereotypical ways and their insights are ignored. A thoughtful link could be made to other groups in society whose contributions are often similarly dismissed.

You then explored some aspects of life that adversely affect children's spirituality. I chose to confine our discussion to two contrasting elements. the first was 'toxic childhood syndrome' which describes the corrosive lifestyle of Western society where children 'enjoy' the trappings of modernity but often seem to be lost. Secondly, child abuse was linked to the crushing of the human spirit and I suggested that the long-term damage sustained could be as overt as other more visible aspects of abuse. Using the Victoria Climbié case as a reminder you then looked at how spiritual belief could be misused to abuse children, in particular the trend for children to be branded as demon-possessed and for some religious groups to seek a cure through such methods as beatings and starvation. Not for the first time in this book, you may have thought that religious belief can be something of a double-edged sword: it can be a core component of spirituality and it can also be used as a means to harm and oppress.

You then spent some time looking at the legislative context of children's work and how spirituality sometimes seems to be absent in key policies. Using two key outcomes from Every Child Matters you then thought about what it means for a child to be healthy. I suggested that there are some creative ways in which work can be done with damaged children: the use of stories, life story work and play therapy. All of these activities need to be skilfully undertaken by someone with expertise and all of them have an explicit spiritual component. Finally, you considered children within the care system and their poor outcomes compared with the rest of the population. I reminded you that we need to be balanced when we come across such statistics and to use our understanding of why damaged children perform poorly as a spur to anti-oppressive practice.

FURTHER READING

Adams, K, Hyde, B and Woolley, R (2008) *The spiritual dimension of childhood.* London: Jessica Kingsley.
This is an excellent book which comprehensively explores the spiritual world of the child.

Brett, D (1986) *Annie stories.* New York: Workman Publishing.
Basic text for parents and therapists alike for designing stories to aid children in coping with fears, loss, pain, siblings and other challenges.

Crompton, M (2001) *Who am I? Promoting children's spiritual well-being in everyday life. A guide for all who care for children.* Ilford: Barnardo's.
An excellent resource of both religious and secular ideas as to how spirituality can be woven into everyday work with vulnerable children.

Hyde, B (2008) *Children and spirituality. Searching for meaning and connectedness.* London: Jessica Kingsley.
Part 2 of this book entitled 'The characteristics of children's spirituality' is especially valuable.

Reddie, AG (2001) *Faith, stories, and the experience of Black Elders. Singing the Lord's song in a strange land.* London: Jessica Kingsley.
This book highlights the importance of storytelling in Caribbean culture and recounts how the author developed an oral tradition document to support and sustain intergenerational storytelling.

The *International Journal of Children's Spirituality* is a well established and well regarded publication which is published four times a year. To quote from the publisher's website, the journal 'provides an international, inter-disciplinary and multi-cultural forum for those involved in research and development of children's and young people's spirituality, within which this debate can be addressed and widened.' See **www.tandf.co.uk/journals/carfax/1364436X.html** for further information.

WEBSITES

For those of you who wish to explore the art of storytelling more I suggest that you visit the website of the 'Center for Digital Story Telling' at: **www.storycenter.org**, which explores narration and the use of story.

Conclusion

This book has covered a range of diverse issues connected to our exploration of social work and spirituality. At the core of our journey there have been two underpinning arguments:

- First, the notion that all people regardless of their age, race, ethnicity, gender or ability have got spiritual needs.

- Second, it has been my consistent argument that if social workers do not acknowledge and respect the spirituality of their service users, and seek to understand their own spirituality, that the profession will have failed in its duty to provide person centred holistic care.

In the first part of the book (Chapters 1, 2 and 3) I attempted to explore the basis of spirituality. This was done in a number of ways and you will recall that we touched on the:

- connections, similarities and differences between religion and spirituality.

- historical and contemporary contribution of faith groups to social care provision.

- influence and importance of culture.

- role and different understandings of gender.

- importance of community and how communities could be seen to be spiritually well or unhealthy.

This is by no means an exhaustive list but captures the spirit (if you will forgive the pun) of the introductory chapters.

The second part of the book attempted to provide a more structured discussion of social work practice and spirituality. I found myself returning to the same themes over and over again – the importance of anti-oppressive practice, the role of relationship, skills such as communication and empathy. This serves to highlight the many commonalities that exist between service user groups and how foolish it is to attempt to place them in neat packages. After all, there are few families which do not incorporate adults, children, older people, people with disabilities and so on.

Just to refresh your memory we considered:

- Older people and the pioneering work of Tom Kitwood and John Killick. You considered the 'spiritual tasks of ageing' and used the experience of dementia to exemplify issues around change and loss and the loss of personhood. You may remember that I started by exploring older people and spirituality because of the generic nature of many of the issues raised. After all, there are no service user groups that do not experience change and loss.

- Disability and the way in which disabled people have historically been publicly and professionally disregarded. I then introduced you to the idea of the spiritually aware social worker. Using the case study of Zahra we posed a number of questions around practice and practice skills. I then used the interesting work of Zohar and Marshall to encourage you to think about the organisation you work for and to suggest that you undertook a spiritual evaluation. Finally, I made the point that spirituality and good spiritual care has advantages for both practitioner and service user.

- Mental distress, the concept of spiritual dislocation and the labyrinthal connections between religion/spirituality and mental illness. You then spend some time thinking about the role of spiritual assessment and what this might entail. Increasingly, the assessment of spirituality is a feature of holistic work in health and social care. We may reflect that it is not asking too much for the spiritual needs and perspectives of the service user to be recorded and considered.

- Children and the way in which they seek to express their spirituality. We noted that in many ways there are few differences between children and adults in how spirituality is explored and expressed. You may recall that we said that those elements of life which children find spiritually corrosive (abuse, neglect, dysfunctional relationships, a lack of love, a hostile community, etc.) also hold true for adults as well.

That seems a good place to stop as the statement purely serves to emphasise the initial points I made in this conclusion. I hope that you have enjoyed the book and feel better equipped to explore and incorporate spirituality into your social work practice. Good luck!

References

Ahmadi, F (2006) Islamic feminism in Iran. *Journal of Feminist Studies in Religion*, 22(2), pp33–53.

Alford, H (ed) (1839) *The works of John Donne*, Vol. 3. London: J.W. Parker.

Barker, C (2008) Men, Buddhism, and the discontents of Western modernity. *Journal of Men, Masculinities and Spirituality*, 2(1), pp29–46.

Baskin, C (2002) Circles of resistance: spirituality in social work practice, education and transformative change. *Currents: New Scholarship in the Human Services*, 1(1), pp1–4.

Basset, F and Basset, T (2007) Promoting spirtual well being in the workplace – training and support for staff. In ME Coyte, P Gilbert and V Nicholls (eds), *Spirituality, values and mental health: Jewels for the journey*. London: Jessica Kingsley.

Bergant, D (1994) Biblical reflections on the question of sacramental access. In E Foley (ed), *Developmental disabilities and sacramental access*. Collegeville, MN: Liturgical Press.

Biddulph, S (1994) *Manhood*. Sydney: Finch.

Bourdieu, P (1977) *Outline of a theory of practice*. Cambridge: Cambridge University Press.

Butcher, H et al. (2007) *Critical community practice*. Bristol: Policy Press.

Canda, ER and Furman, LD (1999) *Spiritual diversity in social work practice*. New York: Free Press.

Chatters, LM (2000) Religion and health: public health research and practice. *Annual review of public health*, 21, p335.

Coleman, PG, McKiernan, F, Mills, M and Speck, P (2002) *Spiritual beliefs and existential meanings in later life: The experience of older bereaved spouses*, Research Findings 3. London: Economic & Social Research Council.

Consedine, J (2002) Spirituality and social justice. In M Nash and B Stewart (eds), *Spirituality and social care. Contributing to personal and community well-being*. London: Jessica Kingsley.

Crawford, K and Walker, J (2005) *Social work with older people*. Exeter: Learning Matters.

Daniel, B and Wassell, S (2002) *The early years: Assessing and promoting resilience in vulnerable children*. London: Jessica Kingsley.

Davis, R (1989) *My journey into Alzheimer's disease*. Wheaton, IL: Tyndale.

De Swaan, A (1988) *In care of the state*. Oxford: Blackwell.

Department for Education and Skills (2003) *Every child matters*. Green Paper. Norwich: HMSO; available online at: **www.everychildmatters.gov.uk**.

Department for Education and Skills (2005) *Every child matters outcomes framework*. Available online at: **www.everychildmatters.gov.uk**.

Department for Education and Skills (2006) *Care matters: Transforming the lives of children and young people in care*. Green Paper. London: HMSO.

Department of Health (2007) *Putting people first: A shared vision and commitment to the transformation of adult social care*. London: HMSO.

Dorling, D, et al. (2007) *Poverty, wealth and place in Britain 1968–2005*. Bristol: Policy Press.

Edwards, W and Gilbert, P (2007) Spiritual assessment – narratives and responses. In ME Coyte, P Gilbert and V Nicholls (eds), *Spirituality, values and mental health: Jewels for the journey*. London: Jessica Kingsley.

Fraser, D (1976) *The evolution of the British welfare state*. Basingstoke: Macmillan.

Gilbert, C (2008) *Uncorrected transcript of oral evidence to be published as HC 70-I. House of Commons Minutes of Evidence taken before the Children, Schools and Families Committee, 10 December 2008*. Available at: **www.publications.parliament.uk**.

Gilbert, P (2003) *The value of everything. Social work and its importance in the field of mental health*. Lyme Regis: Russell House.

Gilbert, P (2006) Breathing out – breathing in. In *Reaching the spirit: Social perspectives network studies day, paper nine*. West Sussex: rpm print & design.

Gilbert, P (2007a) Engaging hearts and minds . . . and the spirit. *Journal of Integrated Care*, 15(4).

Gilbert, P (2007b) The spiritual foundation: awareness and context for people's lives today. In ME Coyte, P Gilbert and V Nicholls (eds), *Spirituality, values and mental health: Jewels for the journey*. London: Jessica Kingsley.

Golightley, M (2008) *Social work and mental health*, 3rd edition. Exeter: Learning Matters.

Gregory, A (1997) The roles of music in society: the ethnomethodological perspective. In D Hargeaves and A. North (eds), *The social psychology of music*. Oxford: Oxford University Press.

Hart, T (2003) *The secret spiritual world of children*. Makawao, HI: Inner Ocean.

Hawkins, PW (2004) The Buddhist insight of emptiness as an antidote for the model of deficient humanness contained within the label intellectually disabled. In C Newell and A Calder (eds), *Voices in disability and spirituality from the land down under: Outback to outfront*. Binghamton, NY: Haworth Press.

Hay, D (1985) Suspicion of the spiritual: teaching religion in a world of secular experience. *British Journal of Religious Education*, 7(3), pp140–7.

Hay, D and Nye, R (2006) *The spirit of the child*, revised edn. London: Jessica Kingsley.

Heenan, D (2006) Art as therapy: an effective way of promoting positive mental health? *Disability and Society*, 21(2), pp179–91.

Hillman, S (2002) Participatory singing for older people: a perception of benefit. *Health Education*, 102(4), pp163–71.

Hodge, DR (2005) Developing a spiritual assessment toolbox: a discussion of the strengths and limitations of five different assessment methods. *Health and Social Work*, 30(4), pp314–23.

Jewell, A (ed) (2004) *Ageing, spirituality, and well-being*. London: Jessica Kingsley.

King, U (1993) *Women and spirituality: Voices of protest and promise*. Basingstoke: Macmillan.

Kitwood, T (1997) *Dementia reconsidered: The person comes first*. Buckingham: Open University Press.

Koenig, HG, Larson, DB and McCullough, ME (2001) *Handbook of religion and health*. New York: Oxford University Press.

Laming, H (2003) *The Victoria Climbié inquiry report*. London: HMSO.

Langlands, C, Mitchell, D and Gordon, T (2007) Spiritual competence: mental health and palliative care. In ME Coyte, P Gilbert and V Nicholls (eds), *Spirituality, values and mental health: Jewels for the journey*. London: Jessica Kingsley.

Lewis, DA and Salem, G (1986) *Fear of crime: Incivility and the production of a social problem*. Edison, NJ: Transaction Books.

Lindridge, A (2007) *Keeping the faith: Spirituality and recovery from mental health problems*. London: Mental Health Foundation.

Lippy, CH (2005) *Do real men pray? Images of the Christian man and male spirituality in White protestant America*. Knoxville, TN: University of Tennessee.

Lloyd, M (1997) Dying and bereavement, spirituality and social work in a market economy of welfare. *British Journal of Social Work*, 27(2), pp175–90.

Lyons, K, Manion, K and Carlsen, M (2006) *International perspectives on social work*. Basingstoke: Palgrave Macmillan.

Mental Health Foundation (2007) *Making space for spirituality: How to support service users*. London: MHF.

Mercer, JA (2006) Children as mystics, activists, sages and holy fools: Understanding the spirituality of children and its significance for clinical work. *Pastoral Psychology*, 54(5), pp497–515.

Miller, J (1990) Goodbye to all this. *Independent on Sunday*, 15 July.

Moodie, C (2006) WAGs £1 million pound shopping spree boosts sleepy town. *Daily Mail*, 10 July.

Mosely, E (2004) Solitary confinement in the forgotten ministry. In C Newell and A Calder (eds), *Voices in disability and spirituality from the land down under: Outback to outfront*. Binghamton, NY: Haworth Press.

Moss, B (2002) Spirituality: A personal perspective. In D Tomlinson and W Trew (ed), *Equalising opportunities: Minimising oppression*. London: Routledge.

Moss, B and Thompson, N (2007) Spirituality and equality. *Social and Public Policy Review*, 1.1.

Murray, C et al. (1996) *Charles Murray and the underclass: The developing debate*, Choice in Welfare No. 33. London: IEA Health and Welfare Unit; available online at: **www.civitas.org.uk**

Narayanasamy, A, Gates, B and Swinton, J (2002) Spirituality and learning disabilities: A qualitative study. *British Journal of Nursing*, 11(14), pp948–57.

Neuberger, J (2004) *Dying well: A guide to enabling a good death*. Oxford: Radcliffe Publishing.

Nicholls, V (2007) Connecting past and present: a survivor reflects on spirituality and mental health. In ME Coyte, P Gilbert and V Nicholls (eds), *Spirituality, values and mental health: Jewels for the journey*. London: Jessica Kingsley.

NIMHE/Mental Health Foundation (2003) *Inspiring hope: Recognising the importance of spirituality in a whole person approach to mental health*. Leeds: NIMHE.

NSPCC (2006) 'Emotional abuse survey and debate'. Online at: **societv.guardian.co.uk**

Office of the United Nations High Commissioner for Human Rights (1989) Convention on the Rights of the Child. Available online at: **www2.ohchr.org/english/law**

Palmer, S (2007) *Toxic childhood: How the modern world Is damaging our children and what we can do about it*. London: Orion.

Pointon, B (2007) Who am I? The search for spirituality in dementia. A family carer's perspective. In ME Coyte, P Gilbert and V Nicholls (eds), *Spirituality, values and mental health: Jewels for the journey*. London: Jessica Kingsley.

Powell, A (2007) Spirituality and psychiatry – crossing the divide. In ME Coyte, P Gilbert and V Nicholls (eds), *Spirituality, values and mental health: Jewels for the journey*. London: Jessica Kingsley.

Putnam, R (2001) *Bowling alone: The collapse and revival of an American community*. New York: Simon & Schuster.

Robinson, BA (1999) *The Nottingham UK ritual abuse cases*. Online at: **www.religioustolerance.org**

Robinson, S (2008) *Spirituality, ethics and care*. London: Jessica Kingsley.

Ryan, W (1971) *Blaming the victim*. New York: Random House.

Scott, D (2004) Retrospective spiritual narratives: exploring recalled childhood and adolescent spiritual experiences. *International Journal of Children's Spirituality*, 9(1), pp67–79.

Selway, D and Ashman, AF (1998) Disability, religion and health: a literature review in search of the spiritual dimensions of disability. *Disability and Society*, 13(3), pp429–39.

Shamy, E (2003) *A guide to the spiritual dimension of care for people with Alzheimer's disease and related dementia: More than body, brain and breath*. London: Jessica Kingsley.

Sims, A (2007) *Ups and downs of spirituality in mental health*, Newsletter 23. The Royal College of Psychiatrists Spirituality and Psychiatry interest group; available online at: **www.rcpsych.ac.uk**.

Slay, G (2007) Let's get spiritual. *Mental Health Practice*, 11(4).

Smalley, KJ (2001) Open wide the doors to Christ: persons with intellectual disabilities and the Roman Catholic faith. In WC Gaventa and DC Coulter (eds), *Spirituality and intellectual disability*. Binghamton, NY: Haworth Press.

Sood, MP (2006) Life story. In *Reaching the spirit: Social perspectives network studies day, paper nine*. West Sussex: rpm print & design.

Stacy, R, Brittain, K and Kerr S (2002) Singing for health: An exploration of the issues. *Health Education*, 102(4), pp156–62.

Stobart, E (2006) *Child abuse linked to accusations of 'possession' and 'witchcraft'*, Research Report No. 750. London: DfES. Available online at: **www.dcsf.gov.uk/research/data**

Tacey, D (2004) *The spirituality revolution: The emergence of contemporary spirituality*. Hove: Brunner/Routledge.

Tanyi, R (2002) Towards clarification of the meaning of spirituality. *Journal of Advanced Nursing*, 39(5), pp500–9.

Tearfund (2007) *Churchgoing in the UK: A research report from Tearfund on church attendance in the UK*. Teddington: Tearfund.

Thomas, D (2000) *Dylan Thomas: Collected poems, 1934–1953*. London: Phoenix.

Thompson, N (2001) *Anti-discriminatory practice*. Basingstoke: Palgrave MacMillan.

Thompson, N (2002) Developing anti-discriminatory practice. In D Tomlinson and W Trew (eds), *Equalising opportunities, minimising oppression*. London: Routledge.

Thurlow, R (1999) *Fascism*. Cambridge: Cambridge University Press.

Tomlinson, D and Trew, W (2002) *Equalising opportunities, minimising oppression*. London: Routledge.

United States Conference of Catholic Bishops (2003) *The nature and scope of the problem of sexual abuse of minors by Catholic priests and deacons in the United States,* A Research Study Conducted by the John Jay College of Criminal Justice.

Vanier, J (1995) *Seeing God in others*. Available at: **www.csec.org**.

Vulliamy, E (2006) Welcome to the new Holy Land. *The Observer*, 17 December.

Walsh, K, King, M, Jones, L, Tookman, A and Blizard, R (2002) Spiritual beliefs may affect outcome of bereavement: a prospective study. *British Medical Journal*, 324, pp1551–4.

Warren, J (2007) *Service user and carer participation in social work*. Exeter: Learning Matters.

Williams, P (2009) *Social work with people with learning difficulties*. 2nd edition Exeter: Learning Matters.

Zohar, D and Marshall, I (2004) *Spiritual capital: Wealth we can live by*. San Francisco, CA: Berrett-Koehler.

Index